PREFACE

Fashion keeps on changing but the elements and principles of design remain constant.

The book is designed to provide uninitiated readers with the background necessary for an understanding and appreciation of **Fashion and Apparel Designing Theory**. Topics are systematically divided into two sections; Origin of Fashion, Elements and Principles of Designing, the Biographies of International Designers and their Famous Labels and Fashion in **Chinese Revolution** are covered in Section I. The second Section has been devoted to the treatment of **Prints,** and **Basic Silhouettes,** a knowledge of which is essential before a more comprehensive study of fashion concepts can be undertaken.

I hope that this work would be useful for students both, at Degree and Diploma levels, as well as general readers. It should stimulate, inspire and encourage further study.

I acknowledge my indebtedness and express my gratitude to my parents Mr. P.G. Jayaram and Sulochana, husband Mr. S. Neelesh, colleagues, students and Mr. V.R. Babu (New Age International Publishers) for their help in successfully bringing out this book.

I am thankful to the Principal and Vice-Principal of T. John College and also to my in-laws, Mr. E. Subramani and Pushpavathi, S.

SUMATHI, G.J.
M.A. D.CD & DM
HOD Dept. of F.A.D.
T. John College, Bangalore

PREFACE

Fashion keeps on changing but the elements and principles of design remain constant.

The book is designed to provide immaculated readers with the background necessary for an understanding and appreciation of fashion and Apparel Designing Theory. Topics are systematically divided into two sections. Origin of fashion, Elements and Principles of Designing, the Biographies of International Designers and their Famous Labels and Fashion in Chinese Revolution are covered in Section I. The second Section has been devoted to the treatment of Prints, and Basic Silhouettes, a knowledge of which is essential before a more comprehensive study of fashion concepts can be undertaken.

I hope that this work would be useful for students both, at Degree and Diploma levels, as well as general readers. It should stimulate, inspire and encourage further study.

I acknowledge my indebtedness and express my gratitude to my parents Mr. G.S. Jayaram and Sulochana, husband Mr. S. Neelesh, colleagues, students and Mr. V.B. Babu (New Age International Publishers) for their help in successfully bringing out this book.

I am thankful to the Principal and Vice-Principal of St. John College and also to my in-laws, Mr. K. Subramani and Pushpavathi, S.

SUMATHI, G.J.
M.A., D.F.D. & D.M.
HOD Dept. of F.A.D.
St. John College, Bangalore

Elements of Fashion and Apparel Design

SUMATHI, G.J.

HOD Dept. of F.A.D.
T. John College, Bangalore

PUBLISHING FOR ONE WORLD

NEW AGE INTERNATIONAL (P) LIMITED, PUBLISHERS
New Delhi • Bangalore • Chennai • Cochin • Guwahati • Hyderabad
Jalandhar • Kolkata • Lucknow • Mumbai • Ranchi

Visit us at www.newagepublishers.com

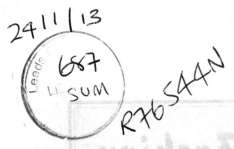

Published by New Age International (P) Ltd., Publishers
First Edition: 2002
Reprint: 2010

Branches:
- No. 37/10, 8th Cross (Near Hanuman Temple), Azad Nagar, Chamrajpet, **Bangalore** - 560 018.
  Tel.: (080) 26756823, Telefax: 26756820, E-mail: bangalore@newagepublishers.com
- 26, Damodaran Street, T. Nagar, **Chennai** - 600 017. Tel.: (044) 24353401, Telefax: 24351463
  E-mail: chennai@newagepublishers.com
- CC-39/1016, Carrier Station Road, Ernakulam South, **Cochin** - 682 016. Tel.: (0484) 2377004, Telefax: 4051303
  E-mail: cochin@newagepublishers.com
- Hemsen Complex, Mohd. Shah Road, Paltan Bazar, Near Starline Hotel, **Guwahati** - 781 008.Tel.: (0361) 2513881
  Telefax: 2543669, E-mail: guwahati@newagepublishers.com
- No. 105, 1st Floor, Madhiray Kaveri Tower, 3-2-19, Azam Jahi Road, Nimboliadda, **Hyderabad** - 500 027.
  Tel.: (040) 24652456, Telefax: 24652457, E-mail:hyderabad@newagepublishers.com
- RDB Chambers (Formerly Lotus Cinema)106A, 1st Floor, S.N. Banerjee Road, **Kolkata** - 700 014.
  Tel.: (033) 22273773, Telefax: 22275247, E-mail:kolkata@newagepublishers.com
- 16-A, Jopling Road, **Lucknow** - 226 001. Tel.: (0522) 2209578, 4045297, Telefax: 2204098
  E-mail: lucknow@newagepublishers.com
- 142C, Victor House, Ground Floor, N.M. Joshi Marg, Lower Parel, **Mumbai** - 400 013. Tel.: (022) 24927869
  Telefax: 24915415, E-mail: mumbai@newagepublishers.com
- 22, Golden House, Daryaganj, **New Delhi** - 110 002. Tel.: (011) 23262370, 23262368, Telefax: 43551305
  E-mail: sales@newagepublishers.com

ISBN (10): 81-224-1371-4
ISBN (13): 978-81-224-1371-7

Rs. 225.00

C-10-08-4885

Printed in India at Ajit Printers, Delhi.

PUBLISHING FOR ONE WORLD
NEW AGE INTERNATIONAL (P) LIMITED, PUBLISHERS
4835/24, Ansari Road, Daryaganj, New Delhi-110002
Visit us at **www.newagepublishers.com**

CONTENTS

SECTION I : Fashion   1-154

1. Fashion ... 3
2. Elements of Fashion ... 10
3. Fashion Industry Language Guide ... 17
4. Fashion Terminology ... 20
5. Elements of Art and Principles of Design ... 31
6. Colour ... 39
7. The Psychology of Clothing ... 46
8. Some Traditional of Textiles of India ... 51
9. Costumes and Fashion ... 66
10. Terms Used for Clothing During French Revolution ... 70
11. Fashion Industry ... 99
12. Fashion Promotion ... 106
13. Fashion Designers and Their Famous Labels ... 111
14. History of Costumes ... 130
15. The History ... 138
16. Chinese Revolution 16th-21st Century ... 146

SECTION II : Design   155-217

17. Prints ... 157
18. Necklines ... 171
19. Sleeve Styles ... 174

20. Cuffs ... 179
21. Collars ... 182
22. Skirts Shapes and Silhouettes ... 186
23. Basic Silhouettes
24. Pants ... 205
25. Pockets ... 210
26. Hats ... 212
27. Waist Bands ... 214
28. Bows and Ties ... 216

SECTION I
Fashion

Fashion

CHAPTER 1

Introduction

What we do and how we live - It's fashion that makes us all perceive. Fashion is forever, but, trends will be new. For who knows just what next will ensue.

You must be aware that over years and centuries, we have lived with fashion. The very word *Fashion* connotes the way of living of each one of us. Whether young or old fashion is what we visualize. It is the inner feeling of every human being to present himself or herself according to one's own thinking. Thought helps us in the grooming of a person. In other words, it protrudes one's lifestyle.

'Fashion' and 'Lifestyle' go hand-in-hand. They are communicated by what we see, and for that colour plays the major part. It emphasises various images and objects in our day-to-day life.

Let us go deeper what we mean by 'Lifestyle'. Each one of us wish to mould our own lives. This depends to a great extent on our moods, whims and fancies. It does not mean that one goes wearing anything at anytime or anywhere. There are various patterns or norms laid by the society and as far as possible, one tries to adhere to them. Here also, fashion and society go together. People have become more fashion conscious, mainly because in the competitive world that we face today, we are conscious of society accepting us as we are. We talk more to do with fashion.

We see, hear and live with 'fashion'. Every human being is aware of appearing as the occasion demands. The appearance may be simple or elaborate, dull or glittering, dreary or glamourous, sad or happy. Life breathes fashion in every corner of the world. Decades, centuries and era's have seen the changing fashion in the mode of living for instance, in building construction or decoration, apparels, all breath one word *'fashion'*.

Times keep changing and so also fashion. One may be personified old fashioned, traditional, customary, rigid, practical, trendy, sexy, footloose, go-getter or modern generations have seen the colour and glamour that add to 'fashion'. Without fashion, life would not be worth living.

The world of fashion brings delight and comfort to all and talented people enable the world to progress with fashion. What one sees gets communicated with eyes and vision gets translated into words, figures and patterns.

Come what may, 'fashion' leads the world and it will continue to do so through centuries. Life cannot be separated from fashion. Twentieth century has seen marvelous developments in fashion. With the coming of twenty-first century, we envisage tremendous changes - who knows in the computer world, a new innovation may entirely change the fashion arena [this process has already been started].

What is Fashion?

'Fashion' comes from a Latin word 'Facere' which means 'to make'. It carries the idea of craftsmanship and obedience to the Law of technique.

Merle's in 1970's recognized fashion as a concept motivated by change. Ross in 1982 suggested that fashion could be seen as a series of recurring changes in the choice of a group of people. It is marked by rhythmic imitation and innovation, alternative uniformity and change. Fashion is a style that takes place on a body or face or an appearance that varies from person to person, day-to-day, time-to-time. A style which has the capacity to attract and copy is called 'fashion'.

It is the interpretation of the accepted style at any given time. Whenever a style is accepted and worn by sufficient number of people, it is in fashion or it becomes fashion.

Fashion is a natural instinct in people. Men and women are fond of adorning themselves to look more than attractive, to look different, to set an image or style of their own, to be basically an individual, and look different. Variety is spice of life. Love of fashion is deeply seated in human nature, even in the old days regardless of the existence or absence of wealth. Fashion may decree rich clothing, bright colouring, but, when copied to excess they become common and they are no longer in good taste.

The everlasting thirst for clothes has made design play an important role in our lives. Well chosen clothes influence social acceptance as well as the popularity as a person and greatly reflect the self esteem of the wearer, which largely extends an aura of confidence. The choice of cloth is determined by fashion which keeps on changing.

Mass accomplishments are reflected in fashion but fashion itself may not be an important part of cultural environment.

Fashion can be defined in many ways and fashion means 'many things to many people'. It may be "applause", "Golden dream", "Looking good", "Traffic stoppers", "Stroke of genius", "Right of exclusive taste", "The superlatives", "Reviving up to face the future", "Chameleon like creature".

Fashion can be defined as what a specific group of people wear, use during a given time period. This is simple definition. Fashion is human behaviour. Fashion is an art and it is a science. To be more brief it is an artistic science and scientific art of learning to combine colour, form, pattern and texture for the final effect that is right for the time, place and the user.

Historians and fashion experts would probably differ on the words used to define fashion, but, there would be unanimous agreement that the elements of fashion are - People, Acceptance, Time and Place. It follows, therefore, that a fashion is anything that is accepted by a substantial group of people, at a given time, in a given place. One could say that the definition covers an almost infinite range of products, ideas, practices and attitudes. In a broad sense, fashion is the culture of the time; a set of learning beliefs, attitudes, habits and forms of behaviour that are shared by society and are transmitted from generation to generation within that society. The meaning of fashion is so broad that it covers almost every aspect of human behaviour.

The requirement of a substantial group of people is relative. Substantial can be interpreted as a group of people who have influence on others and/or who can obtain the recognition of others.

Fashion is associated with a particular Time or Period. What is important today can be "Old hat" tomorrow. Try this test - watch an old movie on television. The cars, interior and clothes and even acting are out-dated. Out present lifestyle is far removed from what was accepted at the time of the film.

The place strongly affects what is acceptable. Different people in different places have different aspirations, taste, education and experience. Particular groups have particular guidelines for acceptance. It does not take close examination to identify food, fashions and ultimately culture of different countries. Even in India, different regions have different values of fashion apparel, food and life styles. These are referred to as sub-cultural or regional values.

The fundamental characteristics of fashion is acceptance. Styles offered by fashion designers are not fashion until consumers accept them and purchase them.

Origin of Fashion

Fashion previously percolated from the upper class. The lower classes tend to imitate their social superiors. The material and variety of fashion are adopted by each class to suit their own requirements.

Previously, fashion spread vertically down the social hierarchy. Royalty created fashions which were then copied by the lower class. These days people from all classes wear fashionable styles roughly at the same time. What was once the province of minority has become a general acceptance, ordinary people throughout the world are acquainted with the latest fashion in clothing.

How Fashions are Spread?

Formerly fashion spread slowly owing to slow transportation. Such is not the case at present. If, fashion starts at New York, it spreads over the world rapidly through such media as the magazines, newspapers, radio, television, etc.

Launching of a fashion depends mostly on publicity. Sketches in fashion magazines and competitive advertising in the papers are used for fashion publicity. Fashion shows press releases, and publicity material, pass on the fashion theme to the public. Most newspapers and periodicals give some space to fashion. They can be spread if a particular style is being worn by popular figures, celebrated stars, top models, etc. but, there can be no doubt, that media, such as, press, television channels, video, cinema and show (fashion) play a very important role for appealing them to public.

Reasons for Change in Fashion

Human being are inquisitive, and curious creatures, so the fashion changes are motivated by the visual need for a new image. Curiosity, desire to be different, self assertion, rebellion against convention, companionship and intimation are some of the reasons for fashion change.

For many years, there has been change of fashion from season to season because of temperature and weather change, but, now styles change more frequently, largely because of our in-born desire for something new.

Fashion, a governing factor has had both direct and indirect impact on teenage group especially the college going class, creating waves of changes.

The Design

Design is Organisation. When anything is designed, it is "put together with same intent or goal in mind". Everything that is not entirely accidental is to some extent, DESIGNED.

Music is designed, coffee is designed, marriages are designed, so are books about design, pocket calculators, jokes and fire crackers. Some designs are utterly simple, some astoundingly complex, some succeed, other fail. Whenever some thing is purposely done, some one has "Designed" it.

Some designs are casual and some are in highly deliberate fashion. Things are almost always designed with more than one purpose in mind. Most fire crackers, for example, are not only designed to explode, they are also designed with safety in mind same way fashion designing is designed with the variety of purpose including new styles and use of innovative materials.

Any arrangement of part, form, colour, fabric and line. For example, to create a version or a style. This definition is applicable for apparel or clothing. In general, design is arrangement or putting out creative ideas on paper or any of the three dimensional form.

The Design Professional

You have come across the word "Design and Designers" very often. You always wanted to know about the design professionals.

The equipment of designers are—the ideas, emotions and experience of life. It is important to remember that all the designers use their basic art skills to pursue career one or in other specialist area. Here are the few professions that are related to the study of art and design.

Industrial Designers are concerned with the appearance and function of consumer products. Their work is mainly three dimensional and the products they design can range from cars, fridges, stereos to perfume bottles and tooth brushes. They are familiar with manufacturing processes and different types of materials from which many modern objects are made.

Graphic designers are also called as visual communicators or commercial artists. Their job is to design all types of printed matters, such as, posters, stamps, magazines, books, packages and wrapping papers.

They also work out signs and symbols. Their aim is always to present information as clearly and attractively as possible. Graphic artists have to combine their artistic experience with a technical knowledge of printing procedures. Some may specialize in illustration work, many work in advertising.

Textile Designers are concerned with the designs of fabrics for a variety of purposes from clothes to carpets. They must understand the nature of their materials and acquire technical experience in dyeing, weaving and printing. Colour, shape, texture and pattern are the key elements in textile design.

Fashion Designers anticipate the latest fashion trends and design clothes for particular needs. They must have knowledge of the use of fabrics, of pattern making and manufacturing methods and the skill to communicate their ideas through sketches and drawings.

Other art students take up careers like, jewelry designers, ceramic designers; some become art or craft teachers; and, yet others may enter the field of interior design or designing for stage, film, and television productions, either sets or costumes. Professions from allied fields of study include architecture, gallery and museum administration and photography.

What is Fashion Designing?

Design is concerned with how needs are identified, related and in some cases stimulated. It affects the ways in which our materials, energy, skills and other resources are employed to satisfy them fully, it calls upon enterprise and enthusiasm, inventiveness and ingenuity, scientific discovery and technical knowledge, power of visualisation together with knowledge of human capabilities and aesthetic sensibility. Designing requires patience and planning. Many youngsters want to get finished with their designing sooner than they start. They do not devote their attention to the preliminary procedures, and in many cases a job is left half done to start a new one. Instead with a little more patience and perseverance, you will feel very proud of having produced something beautiful and original and that will be a real stimulating experience.

Creating or styling the appearance of a person with reference to clothing, accessories and beauty in corresponding with the personality of any individual is fashion designing.

Fashion designing involves knowledge of basic elements of designing, understanding colour cycle, brief study of history of clothing, knowledge of fibres and different fabrics - textiles, trims and embellishment, garment making and personal grooming.

To be a successful professional in the field of fashion designing knowledge of the above is essential. In following chapters, these points are taken as basic considerations and elaborated likewise with reference to fashion industry.

Why Fashion Concept is Necessary?

Have you ever looked at the clothes you wear? Why they have their shapes? How they are designed and put together?

Clothes are a part of our life. They protect us, warm us and give us pleasure. They express our moods and our personality.

There are four main reasons for wearing clothes:

Firstly, comes modesty, the need to hide one's body from the sight of others. This can be done very easily, and cannot by itself account for all the changes of fashion through the ages. In any case, ideas of what is right and wrong in dress vary from country to country.

Secondly, it protects against the cold or wet, or, in tropical lands, against heat.

Perhaps, the most protective clothing ever devised was a suit of armour, though, by the 15th century this had become so heavy that the knights who wore it, had to be hoisted on their horses by crane.

In modern times, with so many materials to choose from and jobs to be done, protection is usually "built-in" to special clothes designed for the purpose. We see this in the overall of factory workers or the helmets worn by miners, steel workers and racing drivers. The most complicated protection of all is the space suit.

Thirdly, is utility - for instance the need to carry things. This has influenced the shape of clothing. Since pockets were first designed in the 17th century, they have been incorporated into every type of dress. Women get over this by carrying hand bags, but, they only started to do so when the skirts became too tight to allow pockets.

Fourthly, comes the most important one of all is variety - the urge to decorate and adorn one's person, to be different, and to appear more attractive than others, being different also increases their pride and self-confidence. Even people who wear little or no clothing, like the ab-origins of North Australia, paint tattoo, or scar their bodies with complicated patterns of decoration (in one part of Burma, there are so called "giraffe-necked" women who stretch their necks with high collars of brass rings).

People from every where can share tastes and fashions, receiving few of them as they have happened. When a new style appears it is seen and copied all over the world. What the statesman or celebrity wears one day will be prepared for mass production, the next.

The clothes what we design should be practical. They must be comfortable, light, yet warm as per weather requirements.

Fashion designer must be capable of interpreting the taste of the present era and then guide and condition it with their creations.

A designer often gets inspired by the post-civilization and great artistical works. It was Poiret who put a final clause to corset and introduced the youthful figure which is a total 20th century idea. His clothes were the long loose and flowing, once inspired by classical Greek costumes and also free flowing tunics work by Isadora Duncan. On the other hand, his rich silk and velvets were inspired by the orient. It was Poiret who revolutionized the art of fashion. He commissioned talented artists like, Paul Iribe, George Lapape, to illustrate his designs and soon the fashion magazines were graced with elegant drawing sporting the latest look. Today fashion drawings are largely replaced by photography, but most are boring repetitions and are limited chiefly to fashion journals. Always unvarying, monotonous faces and lighting.

For a designer, everything must come about naturally. Fabric colour, lines sketching plays important part in designing. It is very perplexing to transfer a feeling of atmosphere in the form of a sketch and make it alive and positive establishing a proper balance between technique and industrial demand. It is easier to design ones own fabrics and then create, thus bringing about a pleasing co-ordination between the fabric and line.

Elements of Fashion

CHAPTER 2

The nature of fashion demands are far more complex that most people realise. A fashion professional knows fashion apparel as a unique product; one that reflects self-concept, life-style, change, time and place. Above all fashion is a result of acceptance.

Classification of Fashion

The duration of fashion's importance is a critical fashion designers or manufacturers concern. A fashion can be brief or of long duration. Once having identified this characteristic, a designer is in a position to assess a fashions importance to the retail inventory.

Fashion is classified into many types, such as:

a) Style

b) Basic or classic

c) Fashion Trend

d) Fad

e) Fashion Forecasting

a) Style

Style is always constant. It does not change whereas fashion changes. It is not constant. It is the modification of fashion. Style is the basic outline of any garment. When we add a different neckline and different sleeves with some trimming here and there over a basic garment then the basic garment is modified into a different look or a different outfit, this modification garment will become fashion, when it is accepted by people.

The term style is a popular word in fashion and refers to a sub-division within fashion. By definition, it is that which has certain characteristics that distinguish it from other designs. For example, the fashion could be pleated skirt, yet the style is box pleat. It is a common fallacy to believe that the famous designers create fashions. They create styles which they hope will be accepted. When and if there is consumer support the styles then becomes fashion. It is repetitious but important to stress that fashion is synonymous with acceptance.

b) Basic or Classics

When a fashion is constant or long lasting, such as, *salwar kameez* and saree, it is called Basic or Classic. It is similar to a standard music. The *salwar kameez* and *saree* are part of fashion scene. A customer has one or more in her wardrobe, to be worn to suit different occasions. In certain times, the basics becomes the most important promotable fashion, but, in or out, they remain as a part of the fashion scene. There are many outfits that fall into this classification, such as, *chudidhar*, *kurta*, *dupattas*, shirt and trousers, plain or pleated skirts and denims, etc. there are general fashions that lasts for years, such as, the *saree*, the single breasted men's suit.

Basics or Classics are the outfits which stays in the fashion scene for a long period of time that is from past to present and even in future it stands.

When we watch old movies as well as the new movies which is released just, we can see the *saris* and *salwar kameez* worn in it may be with a slight change or modification accordingly.

c) Fad

A Fad is something which can either make a designer's life more interesting or more tense. Very often something appears on the fashion scene that captures the imagination, only to fizzle out in short duration.

Overall, Fad can be defined as short lived fashion, lasting for a very little time or period, acceptable by only a certain group of people. For example, hippies - their clothing, accessories, hairstyles, etc.

As Fad is short lived fashion, it stays for a very short period, because they are very costly and every one cannot afford to buy it. For example, *dhoti salwar*, tube skirts and so on.

A fashion expert is a selector for consumers - selecting what is more likely to be accepted going overboard for short lived fashion - Fad can be costly.

d) Fashion Trend

There are certain outfits which are in fashion now. The garment which are currently in fashion scene are called fashion trend. This will be changing very often. They are not as costly as Fad. The garment which is liked by many people will be stitched bulky using better quality of fabric and trimming and sold in the market, so that the garments are not only bought and worn by the upper class, it can also affords the middle class, and then these dresses become fashion trends. For example, *salwar* suits, parallels, *salwar* and short tops, and so on.

e) Fashion Forecasting

This is the important part of fashion scenario because when any new garment is designed by the designer and worn, it will not create fashion by itself. It needs the media to spread fashion and this media which spread fashion and gets the fame and name to the designers is Fashion Forecasting.

Fashion Forecasting is done through many communicating media, such as, cinema, fashion shows, press, magazines, newspapers and window display.

Fashion Forecasting is done where crowd is formed in such occasion, so that it can create fashion.

Fashion is Cyclical

The term fashion cycle is termed as a Process involving form the beginning, the rise to the peak of popularity and finally to the decline and abandonment of it. This movement has important meaning to the fashion business. The dynamics of fashion apparel as well as the relationship of:

— the movement of fashion

— the acceptance of group

— the price ranges.

In this evolution, the fashions at the highest prices are adopted by the early acceptors and purchased at stores with fashion leadership. If the fashion moves up, it is accepted by early followers and much larger group than early acceptors and purchased at departmental stores stocking medium to high priced goods. Later, when fashion moves further up the peak, it is accepted at the broadest acceptance level, by the largest consumer group, and obtainable in the widest possible number of retail establishment at lower prices. After the peak, the fashion becomes available at the cheapest prices often stocked at mark down racks and in some stores at low promotional price levels before abandonment.

Fashion is not a price, it can rise from any price level. However, new fashions often start at higher price and then trickle down to acceptance by wider segments of the population at lesser prices.

What Influences Fashion?

As discussed, if fashion is a reflection of our life styles, there are certain factors in our lives which influence it. The broad influences that motivate people to purchase fashionable items are-

→ Economics

→ Social Activities

→ Cultural Activities

→ Technology

→ Political Activities

Economics

Now matter how one approaches fashion. The conclusions drawn are luxury. We do not buy a garment when it is not a fashionable item, even though, it may be cheaper, however, a fashionable outfit will be costlier in contrast to this. This leads to a conclusion that a group of people who are economically sound buy fashionable articles which are quality products also. These designs are imitated on cheaper fabrics for a lower class of people. However, merchandise products must have acceptance value. Mass fashion production succeeds when the right styles are produced at right prices for wide acceptance.

Social Activities

The social attitudes of a country have a strong effect on its fashion institutions. Opening night of an Opera or Derby events are examples of social events that usually merits coverage by the press, of who attended and what they wore. This news is devoured by the public, anxious to see what society leaders accept as the appropriate dress for such an occasion. More social activities require more clothing, the right clothing for the occasion. Casual wear and active sportswear are the most important components of an individual's wardrobe.

We have accepted them as part of our lifestyles, a way that allows us to dress as we please for almost any function. The casual attitude about clothing standards has not only given fashion marketers wider opportunities, but also helped to democratize clothing.

Cultural Activities

The cultural activities of people are reflected in their art forms. Clothing can be considered as an art form. It has shape, colour and arrangement of details i.e., design. This finished product should look as aesthetic as a painting what people appreciate and accept depend upon their aesthetic values, shaped by their education, interest and exposure to art forms.

In India, we have arts and crafts - such as, folk singing, handicrafts, weaving and pottery which have unique cultural values. An abundant need to learn and impart our cultural heritage and our freedom for doing our "own thing" are influences that spill over into the fashions of our clothing. The result of which is that we developed, accepted and became internationally famous for some of the prints/textiles, like, *Bandhini*, Madras checks cotton, dobby, silk, etc. Some apparels like, *saree*, Nehru waistcoat, Jodhpur slacks, etc. are a few of the Indian costumes accepted world wide. Our designers are in the vanguard of the fashion world when the ethnic look assumes international importance and the most important ethnic style which has all combinations of casual, active or partywear of all times is the *salwar-kameez*.

Technology

We are living in a world of new technology. The wonderful world of chemistry has produced nylon, acrylic, polyester and a combination of man-made fibres with natural fibres. In otherwords, we lived in a world of synthetics. Man-made fabrics now rule the textile industry. Although, it is indisputable the natural fabrics, such as, wool and cotton are in the spotlight of fashion importance, but, at prices they generally make them a part of better priced merchandise. Technological strides inherent in clothing which is only one phase of science in our study of fashion. New places, exposure to different ideas and familiarity with foreign customs broadens one's scope and lays the ground work for wider acceptance of art forms and fashions. How can one deny the softness of Scottish cashmere, the suppleness of Spanish cape skin, the beauty of Italian shoes and handbags - just to mention a few popular categories, that have become important to the Indian fashion scene. All this has become easily accessible and more knowledge can be gained through science and technology which have produced aeroplane and television. This exposure helps to internationalize fashion.

Political Activities

Political activities can inhibit or enhance the fashion of the times and is probably an influence not often considered. The most obvious examples are restrictions which take place during wars, when the Government dictates the amount of fabric to be used in garments in order to preserve textiles in an attempt to save fabric. It is interesting to note that men lost their vests and pants, cuffs, during World War-II. Previously, suits were offered with both features and commonly with two paved way pairs of pants. World War-II activity made for many fashions, some of which have become classic-chino pants, combat boots, field jackets and caps were few items that caught the imagination of civilian population.

Today, the cost and degree of exports and imports are regulated by Government. If laws are enacted to curtial quantities of merchandise leaving the country [by embargo's], it can cause an unlimitation on what is available in stores, exports/imports can be a competitive factor for domestic products and tend to depress some domestic retail price level.

These broad areas of influences are exerted on a constant basis, though, we usually do not associate our wearing apparel with them. We are more prone to realise specific causes, such as, influence of film as a medium and imitation of film stars.

Fashion is a vast industrial project for any fashion designer. Most of the designers make careful study of what is currently in demand and based on their findings build a framework for the future. A fashion designer should know that the fashion changes through evolution; that a drastic change may cause resistance. Their practice should be to newer version and to probe with more daring styles which could provide clues to probable acceptance. Consumer acceptance behaviour for fashion apparel is motivated by a search to seek a state of betterment.

Creating Fashion Illustration
(Fashion Creation)

Factors Considered While Designing Fashionable Dress

Among the factors which needs consideration in designing a dress are the age, sex, figure and personality of the wearer, occasion and the purpose for which the dress has to be worn, and the amount of money on wearer would like to spend on it, are the most important. The design should conform generally to fashion trends (current fashion) and still it should look individualistic. If the fabric has been bought before deciding the design of the dress, then plan the dress design to suit its colour, print and texture of the material as well as the amount of material on hand. Make yourself familiar with the basic style and silhouette of dresses before venturing into designing. You must recognize the best lines, such as, vertical, horizontal, oblique, curved, etc. and shapes such as, circular, oval, square, triangle, tubular, etc. for various figure types. You should also endeavour to combine colours and textures in an artistic manner.

Design the structural design details in a dress such as, yokes, pockets, collars, ties, belts, cuffs, sleeves, etc. so that they are well spaced and harmoniously related to the silhouette of the dress and the figure of the wearer. Plain decorator details and trimmings like, frills, tucks, embroidery, applique, lace etc. to suit the design of the dress and take special care not to overload a dress with decorations.

To be able to combine the basic elements of design, namely, colour, line, texture, shape and form so as to produce charming, interesting and graceful effects, one must necessarily have a knowledge of the principles of art or design classified commonly as harmony, proportion, balance, rhythm and emphasis. These principles will help you to create designs of good taste (if applied with imagination) and to evaluate designs critically.

How can you develop taste, imagination and ability to create your own design? First of all, you must collect design ideas by going through fashion magazines, books with historic costume plates, books with pictures of national and peasant costumes, tribal costumes, etc. You can also observe costumes displayed in museums, dresses of people in famous portraits and current styles displayed at ready-made shops and worn by well-dressed people whom you see at movies, parties, shops, functions, etc. Close observation trains the eye to distinguish distinctive designs from common place designs and good designs from bad ones.

Secondly, you must learn to sketch designs to start with. Using a tracing paper you can trace carefully and exactly few designs from current fashion magazines or pattern books. Later, practice free hand drawing first by looking and copying the designs on hand and next by observing each design carefully and then sketching it from memory. After you have trained yourself to do this, you will be able to put down on paper designs of dresses you may have observed while doing window shopping, while attending some social functions, etc.

Thirdly, develop the ability to evaluate or judge design by critically analysing their design details, decorative details, and style lines in relation to the design of the dress and the personality of the wearer keeping in mind the art principles.

Fourthly, train yourself to observe a design and modify it or adopt it to suit current fashions for different types of personalities, different age groups, sex, occasion and purposes. From one design idea, try to sketch about ten designs with slight variations.

Finally, make an attempt to create your own designs by putting on paper sketches from your imagination which should have been enriched now by the practice you had in observing and sketching a variety of designs.

Fashion Industry Language Guide

CHAPTER 3

◆	Accessories	All articles ranging from hosiery to shoes, bags, belts, gloves, scarves, jewellery and hats worn to complete the enhance of the outfit.
◆	Accessorising	The process of adding accessory items to apparel, on request.
◆	Adaptation	The design that reflects the outstanding features of another design but not an exact copy.
◆	Advertising	A non-personal method of influencing sales through a paid message by an identified sponsor. Advertising appears in media such as newspaper, magazines, television and window display etc.
◆	Apparel	An all embracing term that is applied to men's, women's and children clothing.
◆	Avant-garde	In any art, the most daring of experimentalists, innovation of original and unconventional designs, ideas or techniques during a particular period.
◆	Boutique	A free standing shop devoted to specialized sales for the customer with special interest.
◆	Classic	A particular style that continues as an accepted fashion over an extended period of time.
◆	Collection	A manufacturer's or designer's group of styles and of design creations for a specific season. The seasons total number of styles of designs, accumulate for presentation to buyers, comprises a collection.
◆	Contractor	A manufacturing concern that does the sewing for other producers. (So called because this work is done on a contractual arrangement).
◆	Cost price	The price at which goods are billed to a store, exclusive of any cash discounts that may apply to the purchase.

◆	Couturier	French word for (male) designer, usually one who has his own couture house.
◆	Couturiere	French word for a female designer one who has her own boutique.
◆	Craze	A fad of fashion characterized by much crowd excitement or emotion.
◆	Custom made	Apparel made to order for an individual customer, out and fitted to individual measurements as opposed to apparel that is mass-produced.
◆	Design	An arrangement of parts, form, colour, fabric, line and texture. Example — to create a version or a style.
◆	Designer	A person who manipulates and arranges fabric, colour and line. Or a person who designs dresses (Illustrations)
◆	Display	A visual presentation of merchandise or ideas.
◆	Fad	The fashion which lives for a short period.
◆	A Fashion or (Fashions)	The particular style(s) is followed and accepted by many people then it is fashion.
◆	Fashion	A continuing process of change in the styles of dresses that are accepted and followed by a large segment of the public at any period of time.
◆	Fashion Consultant	A person who give professional guidance, fashion advice or services.
◆	Fashion Coordinater or (Director)	A person charged with the responsibility for keeping abreast of fashion trends and developments and acting as a source of fashion information to others.
◆	Fashion Cycle	A term that refers to the rise, popularisation and decline of a fashion.
◆	Fashion forecast	A prediction of fashions and styles that will be popular in future.
◆	Fashion Image	The impression the customer has of a retailers position on fashion leadership, quality selection, prices and personality.
◆	Fashion Press	Reporter of fashion news for Magazines, Newspaper and broad casts media such as Radio, TV, Cinema and Audio Visual and Internet.
◆	Fashion show or showing	Formal presentation of a group of styles or collections, often in connections showing the seasons new fashionable outfits created by fashion designer.
◆	Fashion trend	The direction in which the fashion is moving or those styles which are currently in fashion.
◆	Garment Industry	Synonym for the apparel industry.
◆	High fashion	A fashion that is in the stage of limited acceptance.
◆	Hot number	The style number that sells quickly *abd* in sizable quantities.
◆	Haute Couture	The most important high fashion design houses in Paris/French term used

		for the high fashion design houses.
◆	Knock off	A design that is the copy of higher prices garment.
◆	Line	A collection of styles designed for a season.
◆	Line for the line copy	Exact copy of a style originated by a foreign couturier.
◆	Market	Potential customers for a product or service. A store's trading area, a city in which the showrooms of producers are concentrated. The period during which lines are first presented.
◆	Mark up or Mark on	The difference between the billed cost price and the original price of the merchandise
◆	Mass fashion (volume fashion)	Styles or design that are widely accepted and that therefore be produced and sold in large quantities.
◆	Mass production	Production of goods in quantity at fashion Industry.
◆	Openings	Fashion showing of a new collection by apparel producers at the beginning of a season.
◆	Open-to-Buy	The amount of money that a buyer may spend on merchandise to be delivered in a given month.
◆	Pret-a-Porter	Its a french term which means ready to wear apparel, as distinguished from couture clothes, which are custom made.
◆	Ready to wear	Apparel that is mass produced as opposed to apparel made to order (custom made)
◆	Recorder number	A style number that continues to be ordered by sellers and consumers.
◆	Resource	A retailer's term for wholesale suppliers.
◆	Sample	The garment model (may be original in design, a copy or adaptation) to show to the trade.
◆	Style (Noun)	A type of product that can be easily differenciated from another because of its characteristics.
◆	Style (Verb)	To give a particular characteristics to a group of garments for example — a line of gowns.
◆	Style (Number)	Give to a design by a manufacturer. These numbers are given to the retailers rescue which helps him to order or identify a particular item or garment.
◆	Stylist	One who advises, converting styles in clothes, finishing and so on.
◆	Trunk Show	Designers complete collection displayed in a store for the customers to see and order the style numbers for themselves so that a similar outfit can be designed in their size.

Fashion Terminology

CHAPTER 4

◆ According pleats	Fold of 1/4" to 3/4" in cloth.
◆ Achromatic colour	Black or white; a non-colour.
◆ Advancing colours	A colour that appears to come forward in a pattern e.g., — red, yellow.
◆ African print	A dynamic and colourful-print, taken from traditional African dress and textiles.
◆ All-weather coat	A coat which can be worn for all weathers. (Any season)
◆ Alpaca	Cloth woven from the brown or black wool of a South American mammal called Alpaca.
◆ American style	In contrast to European or Japanese styles; typically this style is easy going like sporty and casuals.
◆ Animal print	Print taken from skin texture of an animal or its foot prints e.g., snake skin, paw spots.
◆ Antique	A style of the past that describes ancient designs that makes us wonder.
◆ Apparel Industry	The enterprise which manufacture garments.
◆ Arabesque	A style of cloth which has prints connected with Abstract, geometric or swirling motif.
◆ Argyle	A Scottish pattern of diamond shapes often used in socks and sweaters and comes only in three basic colours.
◆ Army look	The shape or colour which resembles the army uniform.
◆ Art deco	The decorative and fine art movement that began in France and England in the early 1920's. Characterised by stylish, geometric

patterns the typical colours used are purple, yellow, green, gold, silver and black.

◆ Art nouveau — Decorative and fine art born in France, Germany and Australia in late 19th century. Linear and curvilinear designs used to crafts and buildings, example—Paris subway stations.

◆ A symmetry — Unbalanced designs where both side (opposite) sides look alike.

◆ Backless — Exposing the back used to describe the dress design e.g., Swim suit.

◆ Baggies — Pants that are fitted at the waist and hips but full in the legs; it is adapted from European styles of seventies.

◆ Bandanna — A cotton scarf with paisley or calico patterns; derived from the term for a particular method of dyeing cloth in India (*Bandhani* print).

◆ Basic Colours — In determining colour schemes, one of the major colours to choose from—often black, white or grey.

◆ Bell Bottom — A pant which is tight from waist to knee and flared at bottom or sweep which was popular in 70's.

◆ Blazer — A long sleeved sports jacket with lapels; sometimes with a crest on the breast pockets.

◆ Bleached — Whitened; describing the clothes from which all colours have been removed e.g., Bleached-out jeans.

◆ Blousing — Gathering a blouse or dress at waist.

◆ Blouson — A woman jacket which is drawn at or slightly below the waist.

◆ Border print — A design that runs along the hem.

◆ Bottom — Clothing worn below the waist e.g., pants or skirt.

◆ Bow tie — A small neck tie with loops worn at Neck for both casual and formal wear.

◆ Bulky — Large, loose fitting.

◆ Burberry — A high quality, traditional rain coat manufactured by burberry.

◆ Button-down — Fastened down with buttons.

◆ Camouflage — A design incorporating the army's brown-green, camouflage-print

◆ Career dressing — A dress code for the professional woman, usually a conservative look styled to fit into what was originally "a man's world".

◆ Casual wear — Informal or every day clothing.

◆ Chambray — A smooth cotton fabric woven using two coloured threads.

◆ Channel suit — A womans suit designed by the French designer Gabrielle — "CoCo" Channel; simple skirt and short collarless jacket.

♦	Check on Check	Having various layered check-patterns and colours.
♦	Chic	Stylish or sophisticated.
♦	Chinois	Chinese style.
♦	Cine mode	A style of fashion that originated in the movies.
♦	Circle skirt	Umbrella skirt, a skirt made by cutting the cloth in a circle.
♦	City wear	Street dress that has a sophisticated fashion image.
♦	Classic	Traditional, the dress which are popular for a long time such as *Saree, Salwar Kameez.*
♦	Class print	Patterns such as paisley and foukard, which are not affected by fashion trends.
♦	Cobalt colours	Hot colours which were popular in sixties. High intensive blue, red, yellow and green were the major colours.
♦	Collections	A pre season showing of designers line; usually held twice a year for spring/summer and fall/winter.
♦	Colour Blocking	Placing equal amount of colours side by side within a single garment to make a visual colour statement. Mondrian fine art was the greatest of all color blockers.
♦	Color coordination	The planning of an outfit by considering the relationships of the colours to be worn.
♦	Complex harmony	Harmonious colour schemes created incompatible.
♦	Conservative	Staying away from fashion trends and keeping to traditional styles.
♦	Contemporary	Current; the new look of today.
♦	Continental	Characteristic; new look of today.
♦	Cool colours	Pleasant colour which keeps cool e.g., blue, green and purple.
♦	Corduroy	Derived from the French tern "Cor du roi" meaning cloth of French royalty which is widely used by people of all ages.
♦	Cosmetic colour	The colour which relates with the make up of the face.
♦	Cosmopolitan	Dress of the citizen of the world rather than citizen of one country.
♦	Costume	Dress based on a theme or story.
♦	Costume Jewellery	Inexpensive Jewellery used in a play.
♦	Country look	An appearance evoked by wearing traditional tweeds.
♦	Crepe process	The procedure involved in shrinking the surface of the silk and rayon to create elegant shining.
♦	Crew neck	The round neck of a sweater or a 'T' shirt.

◆	Cullotes	Originally, a short pant worn by men in 17-18th century in France; today it is the divided skirt of the contemporary fashion.
◆	Designer	One who initiate new fabric concepts either by sketching or with actual fabric.
◆	Dolman	A sleeve cut which is very wide at shoulders and tapered at the wrist
◆	Down jacket	A jacket filled with goose or duck down for insulation against cold.
◆	Drape	The way a fabric falls or hangs on the body.
◆	Duffle coat	A short hooded coat fastened with wooden buttons and ropeloops.
◆	Dungaree	A coarse cotton cloth which is used to make work clothes.
◆	Earth colours	Colour related to the brown family e.g., siema, ocher and nature colours such as green.
◆	Electric colour	A brilliant colour.
◆	Elegance	Grace and sophistication in clothing.
◆	Emblem	A symbol or badge.
◆	Ensemble	An outfit with the look of unity and coordination.
◆	Espadrille	A kind of sandal made of hemp and canvas worn by Basque people.
◆	Ethnic	Native or traditional.
◆	Exoticism	Interest in ethnic clothing styles or clothes evoking a foreign land.
◆	Fabric	A cloth which is made up of fibers by weaving, knitting, felting etc.
◆	Fake fur	Artificial fur made from synthetic material.
◆	Fanny wrap	Sash or cloth draped at the hips for elegant streamlined effect.
◆	Fantastic	Imaginary, romantic, dream line.
◆	Fashion Co-ordinator	A specialist in the wearing of fashion clothes.
◆	Fashion-forward	At the forefront of a new fashion trend, also called "advanced fashion".
◆	Fashion Victims	Unfortunate beings who think only about being first in the latest look with little thought given to how the fashion looks on them. These fashion groups usually wear extreme bizarre fashion.
◆	Fifties	Describing fiftie's clothing, which emphasized the silhouette, rock and roll fashion. Typical colours used were pink, black, grey and aqua.
◆	Fisherman knit sweater	Thick, multi-patterned sweater copied from sweaters worn by fishermen in north Europe.
◆	Flannel	A soft cotton weave, usually printed in a striped/checked patterns;

for jackets and pants.

◆ Flapper — In the twenties a woman who was considered daring for wearing different fashions. The bobbed hair style is also called "the flapper".

◆ Flare — Describing bia's-cut clothing that creates a sleek, linear image, e.g., flared skirt.

◆ Folkloric — Characteristics of ethnic styles.

◆ Formal — Describing a dress code requiring evening dress for women, tuxedos for men.

◆ Foulard — A light weight fabric of silk, rayon, etc. Usually printed with small figures such as fleur-de-lis pattern.

◆ Foundation — An under garment to smooth the figure; the basic facial cosmetics.

◆ Garcon look — A boyish fashion worn by women.

◆ Gingham — A plain weave with checks or stripes.

◆ Glen check — A blue and white suit-check for men or women.

◆ Gradations — Shades of colours, unity is created by related shades or contrasting colours.

◆ Gun club checks — A pattern of double check often in white, black and red-brown used for jackets.

◆ Haberdashery look — An appearance evoked by, combining several tailored men's wear prints and textures in one outfit. The jacket and shirt shape suggest men's wear look.

◆ Hand — The texture and weight of a fabric, the quality of the weave.

◆ Haute couture — Literally, "high sewing" referring to the original designs usually custom-made by Saint Laurent or Ungaro of the European fashion houses. Very expensive.

◆ Hawaiian shirt — A short sleeved shirt in bright tropical prints.

◆ High fashion — Haute couture before it becomes current fashion.

◆ High tech — Advanced industrial technology, in fashion, an ultramodern look.

◆ High hugger — Pants or skirt with the waistline resting on the hips, popular in sixties.

◆ Hippie style — Style of the flower children of 60's; characterized by long hair on men and women, beards, blue jeans and psychedelic colours.

◆ Houndstooth — Pointed check patterned fabric woven for men's and women's fashion.

◆ Ichimatsu check — A pattern in which two squares of colours are used alternately in fabric. Also known as benroku pattern derived from the costume of Japanese Kabuki actor Sanagawa Ichimatsu (19th century).

◆	Imitation	A fake or copy, usually of furs or jewellery, cheaper than the real thing, fake accessories and fur are very popular in recent seasons.
◆	Impact colour	Pure colour used to create a shocking effect example a bright red fire engine.
◆	Inner wear	General term used to describe any clothing worn under a coat or jacket.
◆	Iridescent	Showing an interplay of rainbow like colours. A look achieved by weaving two different kinds of fibers such as rayon and polyester.
◆	Ivy league	A popular look for men in the fifties that originated on such campuses as Harvard, Priceton and Yale; a forerunner to the preppie look; a style characterised by button down collar shirts and pants with a small buckle in the back.
◆	Jeans	Originally, work clothes made of denim. In the 60's denim jeans became big fashion and style spread world wide.
◆	Jewel tones	Deep hues of red, blue, green, and purple with the richness and intensity of fine gems.
◆	Jump suit	One piece garment with pants; popular as casual fashion in 70's and 80's.
◆	Jungle print	A pattern depicting African plants, animals or other elements of African culture.
◆	Junk Jewellery	Imitation jewellery; fun accessories.
◆	Khaki	A colour name that means "earth" in Hindi and indicates a dark or greenish yellow; often a military or Safari colour.
◆	Kimono Sleeves	A sleeve with no distinct separation from the jacket or robe; used to describe the sleeve shape of the Japanese Kimono.
◆	Knickers	Knicker blockers. In the 19th century men's short pant designed for bicycle riding; In England knickers are underpants.
◆	Knock-offs	Inexpensive copies of high-priced designer fashion.
◆	Lacy Knit	A weave constructed to imitate the appearance of lace.
◆	Layered	Describing the fashion look in which cloths layers are worn in noticeably different lengths.
◆	Leg warmer	Tube-shaped. Socks worn above the ankle to keep legs warm.
◆	Leatard	A one piece, close-fitting body suit, like a swim suit; used by dancers.
◆	Liberty print	Small flower patterns from the Liberty Company of England.
◆	Lingerie	Women decorative underwear, such as camisole, emphasizing femininity.

◆ Lofers	Slip on shoes without laces.
◆ Lose fit	Too-large clothing, worn intentionally; also associated with the Japanese bag-lady look popular in the early eighties.
◆ Lounge wear	Casual clothes usually worn around the home and not on the street. Popular lounge wear pieces include caftans and long loose-fitting dresses.
◆ Lycee	A fashion look based on the casual clothing of secondary-school age girls, Paris. The look is sweet and stylist and includes a beret, a low-waisted, pleated Jumper and a white blouse with a large collar.
◆ Macrame	Coarse thread knotted to make decorative belts, bags and other things.
◆ Madras	A cotton cloth—first produced in Madras, India, of multicoloured plain patterns. Used to make shirts and skirts. The colour will some times run when the garment is washed.
◆ Maillot	A womens one piece bathing suit having a classic and simple style that is without embellishment and emphasizes the natural shape of the body.
◆ Masculine	Male; describing women's clothes that are tailored to resemble men's.
◆ Marble print	A speckled pattern that imitates natural stone patterns; used in shoes, bags and accessories.
◆ Marine look	An appearance evoked by wearing a sailor suit or any clothing reminiscent of a nautical style; spring/summer fashion employing a sailor collar, anchor or boat motifs and a blue and white colour palette.
◆ Merchandising	The presentation of new products. All aspects of a product, including design, quality and consumer demand must be considered.
◆ Mesh net	A net usually found in summer bags or shoes; can be decorative or functional for ventilation.
◆ Military look	An appearance designed to imitate an element of the military.
◆ Milk tone	A soft off-white, meant to be added to other colours.
◆ Mismatched	Unexpectedly matched. Combinations such as a silk blouse with a leather jacket, lace worn with mannish pants, plaids with tweeds and two different weaves in the same ensemble.
◆ Moccasins	Casual shoes of soft leather; first worn by native Americans.
◆ Mode	Fashion; originally haute couture.
◆ Modernism	Fashion in 20's and 30's that emphasized function.

◆	Mod look	Fashion from London's Carnaby street; marked by flower prints and colour combinations; also Europeans style suit.
◆	Monotone	A single colour; a black or white colour scheme.
◆	Natural colours	Colours, soft in hue and image, relating to beige. Those colours are popular choices for linen and summer fashion. Grey, soft blue, pink, peach, off-white, and beige are the important natural colours.
◆	Natural fibres	Cotton, Silk, wool and linen, all of which occur in nature. The opposite of fibers which are made from synthetics or chemicals.
◆	Neo classic	Designing modern styles that incorporate traditional design ideas.
◆	Neoromanticism	Modern design that incorporate elements of fantasy and imagination.
◆	Neutral colours	Non-colours; colours without hue and visible wave length. Black, white and grey are true neutrals.
◆	New wave	The fashion trends, originating in London that followed pink fashion; emphasis on extreme, brash fashion.
◆	Nostalgia	A longing for the past. A revival fashion evoking images of the 20's 30's, 50's and 60's.
◆	Oxford	Describing cloth that has a diagonal weave and is named for the town and University of Oxford, England. Originally, this cloth was used for the tennis wear of the University team.
◆	Paisley	Printed with leaf patterns. Originally from ancient India and Persia, paisley designs were popularized by 18th centrury.
◆	Panache	Originally, a small feather plume; now, dash or style.
◆	Pastel colours	A pale, soft colour made by adding white to the bright colours.
◆	Pastoral print	A design showing a landscape scene; often used in T-shirt designs.
◆	Patch work	A folk design made from sewing small patches of cloth together, traditionally used for cushion and bed covers but now also used for accessories and embroidered clothes.
◆	Peasant look	An appearance created from a romantic image of simplicity, usually with full skirt and embroidered blouse.
◆	Peter pan collar	A round shirt collar; often used in children's clothing.
◆	Plain	Simple; not decorative, neat.
◆	Polo shirt	Originally, a shirt worn for polo playing; now, fashionable sport wear, often with a small logo on the chest pocket.
◆	Poor (cheap) chic	Fashion created from cheap clothes often from second-hand stores.
◆	Post-moderns	Describing a trend that emphasized decoration, as opposed to modernism's emphasis on function.

◆	Preppie	Son of Ivy league; a collegiate look. Characterized by polo shirts, chinos and navy blazers. Ralph Lauren is the sitting god to the preppies.
◆	Pret-a-Porter	Ready to wear; can be popular styles or haute couture.
◆	Primary colours	Red, yellow and blue. All other colours are derived from these colours.
◆	Print-on-print	Having one pattern printed on a contrasting pattern, for example, flowers on stripes-wearing different patterns together.
◆	Psychedelic	Relating to hallucinatory drugs popular in 60's among hippies and artists. Effects on the fashion world included acidic colours, strange prints and body painting
◆	Pullover	A sweater without buttons.
◆	Pure colour	The clearest colour value.
◆	Raglan sleeve	A sleeve with slanted seams extending from the under arm to the neck; for comfortable jackets and coats.
◆	Receding colour	A dark colour or colour value that appears smaller than it really is because it seems to reduce or minimize.
◆	Regimental stripe	A neck tie design of stripes in the colours of British Military flags; red, blue or green stripes on a dark blue background.
◆	Resort wear	Casual coloured clothes for sunny vacations like T-shirts, shorts, swim suits etc.
◆	Reversible	Wearable with either sides out.
◆	Rugger (rugby) shirt	A long sleeved, horizontally striped shirt worn by rugby players.
◆	Sack dress	Sixtie's style, A loose fitting dress that was slipped on over the head.
◆	Saddle shoes	Two coloured shoes either white with black or brown.
◆	Safari look	A style derived from clothing worn for hunting big game in Africa; a jacket with patch pockets and a belt, usually in khaki coloured fabric.
◆	Sailor collar	A collar that is V-shaped in front and square at back; part of the marine look.
◆	Scottish	Scottish folk styles. e.g., Fair Isle Sweaters.
◆	Secondary colours	The colours which are got by mixing the pair of primary colours of the colour wheel; orange, voilet and green.
◆	Seamless	Garments without seams usually knits.
◆	Seasonless dressing	A dress which can be worn at any season; example: rayon-dress.

◆	Seersucker	Means "milk and sugar". Crinkled material usually made up of linen or cotton; ideal for summer.
◆	Semiformal	Describing a dress code requiring a single or double-breasted black suit for men, an evening or cocktail dress for women.
◆	Shaggy	Long haired–example, angora or mohair.
◆	Shetland	Woolen material ideal for sweater or a coat; produced at Scotland.
◆	Silhouette	The basic outline of the garment.
◆	Slim	Slender.
◆	Slip on	Dress without opening and directly put over the head or shoes without laces.
◆	Slub	To allow the natural character of a fiber to show up in the surface of the weave.
◆	Solid colour	A single colour without print or pattern.
◆	Sophisticated	Urban or stylish.
◆	Spencer	A long sleeve short jacket; worn in 19th century.
◆	Stadium jacket	A sporty jacket, usually made of satin or flannel, with sleeves of contrasting colour.
◆	Stone wash	Repeated washing of fabric to fade the colour; the effect of putting a stone in the washing machine with the clothes.
◆	Strapless	Without straps, a dress having a bare shoulders.
◆	Stylist	A specialist who creates styles or look; different from designers.
◆	Success dressing	Fashion with a yuppie influence for business or professional women.
◆	Summer dark	Dark colours and black used for summer wear.
◆	Surfer look	A popular sport and resort look.
◆	Sweats	Cotton jersey sports wear.
◆	Synthetic fiber	Fiber with no natural origin such as rayon, linen etc. man made fabrics.
◆	Tailored	Fitted garments of wearability.
◆	Textiles	General term for raw material and woven cloth.
◆	Texture	The look and character of the cloths.
◆	Thirtie's fashion	The styles featuring long, slimlines and feminine bia cuts.
◆	Tiered look	A fashion for skirts and dresses composed of bands of gathered cloth.
◆	Tone-on-tone	Slight variation in the shade of a single colour. Patterns are effects created by tints and shades of the same colour.

- ◆ Top — An item of cloth worn above the waist; example, blouse or jacket.
- ◆ Total look — The appearance evoked by wearing a unified, coordinated outfit.
- ◆ Town wear — Street cloths.
- ◆ Transparency — A Texture so fine that it can be seen through, Gauzes and Georgettes are popular examples.
- ◆ Trans sexual fashion — An Unisexual garment; example, jeans and waist coat.
- ◆ Trendies — Fashion groups who slavishly follow every new fashion movements.
- ◆ Tri colour — The colours of the Indian flag.
- ◆ T-shape — A design that streches across the shoulders and tapers downward.
- ◆ Tweed — Rough wool cloth woven for jackets, pants and skirts.
- ◆ Twin prints — Two prints such as stripe and dot that share the same colour combination. Twin prints are often used in the same garments.
- ◆ Vogue — Fashionable. Something that is trendy and very popular.
- ◆ Wardrobe — A dressers cabinet to store cloths in.
- ◆ Warm colours — The colours suggesting an energetic and up beat image; Red, ,Yellow and Orange are warm colours.
- ◆ Water proof — Impervious to water; can refer to clothing or cosmetics.
- ◆ Wrap around skirt — One piece of material that wraps around the lower half of the body and fastens at the waist.
- ◆ Wrap coat — A coat without buttons or fasteners; can be tied with a sash or worn open.

Elements of Art and Principles of Design

CHAPTER 5

Fashion can be defined as a design that is accepted by a given segment of population. Fashion is constantly changing and as a new design becomes popular a new standard of beauty becomes desirable. Often a new fashion begins when the proportion of a garment is altered, for example, a silhouette is changed in width or a skirt is lengthened. Usually when a truly innovative fashion begins, it takes a long time for the general public to retain its eye and develop an appreciation for a new look. As more people wear the item and interpret it in many different ways, the mass of people find it easier to accept the fashion, as beautiful.

Designing means moving from the state of randomness to the higher state of organisation, to create a design or impression or to communicate an important/innovative idea. On the highest level of design is the careful and knowledgeable manipulation of art elements to produce an expressive personal idea.

There are two basic divisions of designing in the field of clothing:

1   Structural designing
2   Decorative designing.

There are two divisions which are often inseparable. They can be defined in other words as factors influencing the design.

Structural design

Includes the all over design of a garment. Its form and shape plus all the details involved in assembling the sections of the garment such as darts, pleats, tucks etc.

Structural design may add a decorative quality if emphasized by colour contrast or row of top stitching to outline the basic garment parts. In apparel, structural design is more important because it is the fundamental component of design.

To draw a structural design a form or human croque is not necessary. These designs are done by the designers in the buying house. In this category the designs are drawn on the specification chart where much trimmings are not used. These designs will be simple and well defined about their construction, colour, thread and trimmings to be used. It will not be draped on the form. It will be spreaded so that the pattern master can create a proper sample according to the specifications mentions such as its measurements, its sweepline (Hemline) its neckline and any other type of cuts used.

Decorative Design

Here it refers to the design which is drawn by the beginner (learners) as well as the boutique designers. These designs needs the basic form or a croque and the designs drawn will be draped over it. It is not produced in bulk so it will have more trimmings, prints, embroidery, buttons (that do not fasten) and tacked on bows. The garment which is designed will be selected by the customer, then it will be stitched and because it is not produced in bulk, it will be very costly, in these designs the fabric, style and colour combinations are described so that one can select the design. In this design category specification charts is not prepared, nor it is stitched for standard measurement. It is the design and outfit is made for an individual costumer.

Basic Silhouettes

The dictionary meaning of the word '"Silhouette" means a dark image outlined against the lighter background. The Silhouette of a garment refers to the outline shape that it gives to the wearer. Silhouette is determined by the texture of the fabric and the cut of the garment, the length and width of the garment, position of waistline length of the shoulder seam etc. A silhouette may be classified as:

— Tubular

— Normal

— A line

— Bell

— Clinging

— Bouffant, etc.

The basic features of a tubular silhouette is a narrow skirt.

A line silhouette is produced by a skirt with a slight flare at the hemline of the garment and it is joined in the sides from the armhole to the bottom hemline without giving the suppression shape at the waist.

The bell silhouette is full skirted. Fullness may be in the form of gathers, pleats or flare. Bell silhouette is classified into two types as:

a) Medium bell silhouette.

b) Extreme bell silhouette.

This extreme bell silhouette is refered as bouffant silhouette. Stiff fabrics like organdie, taffeta, denim produce bouffant effects, because these fabric stands well rather than draping (less fall). While the fabric such as China silk, crepe and chiffon drapes well and gives a good fall on the body (form). So these produces the clinging silhouette because of its clinging characteristic (fall). Thin figures and short figures should avoid extremely tubular or clinging styles as well as extreme bouffant styles.

Elements of Art

In creating a design one of the components which interact is the Art Elements.

The elements and principles of design are flexible and should be interpreted within the context of current fashion. A design can be defined as an arrangement of lines, shape, colours and texture, that create a visual image. The principles of design are the rates that governs how elements are combined. The elements are therefore the raw materials that must be combined successfully.

The following are the different Elements of Art.

Line

Form

Shape

Texture and

Colour.

These elements are considered as " Plastics" in art language because they can be manipulated or arranged by the designer to create a desired illusions.

1) Line

It provides the visual dimensions of length and width. When lines combine, space is enclosed and forms and shapes are defined. Lines offered a path of vision for the eyes when is wearing an object/outfit. The arrangement of lines in clothing design can cause to appear heavier or thinner than what actually is.

1. Horizontal line

2. Vertical line

3. Oblique line

    4. Diagonal line

    5. Curved line etc.

Lines within a garment are created by darts seams and decorative details. Each kind of line produces its own special effect. Straight line's and shapes denote force and strength and have a masculine quality; curved lines are the lines of nature, they are gracefull and gives a feminine effect.

Lines are the greatest devices of fashion designers. Since lines create illusion of height and width, they can be used to one's requirement to tone down or exaggerate a particular figure type.

Vertical lines: These produce an illusion of added height to the outfit design by adding and contrasting coloured vertical band in the centre or a centre panel added with vertical line gives an added height to the outfit. These lines tends to make a short person looks tall.

Horizontal lines: These lines adds width to the garment and decrease the apparent height, for example a wide contrasting coloured belt shortens the height of the figure by cutting the garment into two segments, however the belt has the effect of slimming the waist line, the self coloured will not shorten the height of the outfit as well as the wearer.

Diagonal lines: These lines can add or decrease the height of the wearer depending on their slope. Long uninturrupted diagonals tilting almost vertically are the most lengthening and most dramatic of all lines.

Diagonal lines should be combined with vertical or horizontal lines. If they are used alone for the entire dress the effect will be disturbing.

Curved lines: These lines are more romantic and pensive by nature. Curved lines can be a full circle or may even appear almost straight. Curved lines are considered graceful and feminine, those in a diagonal direction are the most graceful and can be seen in the soft folds of material in a draped dress or a ruffled collar.

Line Movements: The arrangement of vertical, horizontal and oblique lines produce line movements characterised by opposition, transition or radiation.

Opposition: In a design where the vertical line is opposed by a horizontal lines opposing oblique lines are used.

Transition: When one line direction slips smoothly into another, the movement is transitional (e.g., curved lines). Curved lines should not be over done. They are at their best when stiffened by some straight lines, example round yoke with vertical pintucks within it.

Radiation: When a design is created with radiating lines at the neckline, it will attract attention to the face. These radiating lines are produced by stitching decorative darts on the right side of the garment.

Form: It is an object having three dimensions like length, width and depth.

The human body is a form and by viewing it analytically, its various perspectives are revealed. The human form changes visually with clothing, especially as fashion changes.

Shapes: It describes the outer dimensions or contour of an object. Shape also encloses space and imparts a certain character to the object viewed. Through clothing design, the shape of the human body is often revealed in a natural way, but sometimes even distorted. The shape of clothing on a human body, communicates silently, the messages about the wearer.

Every fashion period, a shape emerges slowly or evolved suddenly, whatever it is, every period has a specific shape of garment which once determined can be modified and re-styled for variation in design without changing the basic shape of the garment, it is either flare or tight, circular or straight, a line or raglan. It has been observed that an easy fitting shape of the garment is easily accepted and largely variated as well as has a longevity of stay, where as a tight fitting garment is generally short lived since it is suitable to only perfect figure types. It is therefore advisable that the designer chooses an easy silhouette to keep on creating for a longer duration.

Space: It is generally considered to be the area seen between the shapes. Busy space in clothing becomes distractive and fatiguing to view where an interesting space may go unnoticed or appear monotonous.

Lines in a costume provide a path of vision along which the eye travels. Curving lines relates more naturally to human bodies. Vertical lines tends to slenderize the body. Horizontal lines suggests width.

Both repetition and extreme contrast of a line, shape, space or form produce emphasis.

Colour and Texture: When we talk of principles of designing, or when we start off with a given design theme the first thing to occur to our minds is the colour and texture of the fabric. Every season or now and then a colour emerges in the fashion scene which is decided by the leading manufacturers, exporters and textile experts of the fashion world. It is advaisable to the amateur to work on the colour in vogue; and to add to its creativity, collaborate with a textile designer and develop a new dimension to the existing patterns. To co-ordinate with an idea of creation will be infinite. Also while choosing a colour one must be utmost careful as colour creates the first impression and hence can glorify or destroy one's appearance. Even a simple silhouette may be enhanced by using effective colour schemes. As texture is the feel, drape and degree of stiffness and softness of the fabric, it also creates a visual effect upon the wearer, given a small swatch of fabric, the designer can visualize the texture and the fall of the fabric which helps him to design further.

Principles of Design

The principles of design are useful in creating different forms of expression in an artistic manner, which are pleasing and attractive to the eye. Following are the principles of designing.

1) Balance

2) Emphasis

3) Harmony

4) Proportion

5) Rhythm

Balance: In clothing balance refers to a visual attribution of weight, from a central area. Balance implies a sense of equillibrium. Pleasing balance brings about a satisfying relationship among all design parts to produce visual harmony. In clothing designs, three kinds of balance are observed.

1) **Formal Balance:** Formal Balance occurs when object appears to equalise each other by repetition and arranged at equi-distance from the centre. The upper and lower portions of the design are so arranged, as to give an effect of balance. Thus there should not be the effect of too much of weight at the bottom or a heavy appearance. For example, dark coloured skirt over lighter shade of pants make a short person more shorter.

2) **Informal Balance:** Occurs when objects appear to equalize each other but not through repetition and the arrangement is in an haphazard manner. Here design of different sizes and shapes and of different attractions are arranged. The larger and more attractive designs are kept as far away from the centre. If used correctly, informal designs can be effective in being attractive.

3) **Radial Balance:** Occurs when major parts of the design radiate from the central part. Formal balance is the least expensive to produce apparel in mass production. Informally balanced garment is more difficult to produce. For each section of the garment cuts will have to be probably handled differently.

Emphasis: Emphasis involves the concentration of interest in the selected area of design with other centre of interest subordinated. Emphasis as such, should not be placed at an area that one wishes to minimize attention drawn on. Designers often create emphasis partially through the careful arrangement of line, texture and colours.

It could also be called as focal point. Every design needs some note of interest that catches the eye or attracts the attention on a specific area of the garment. Contrasting colour for example could be used to emphasise an area.

A black dress with white collar and cuffs will direct the eye to the face and hands. There can be several centres of interest although one or two will be more dominant than the others and will arrest the attention longer and draw the eye back to it more frequently than lesser centres of interest.

Some methods of lay emphasis could be

a) Grouping of design units.

b) Using contrast of hues.

c) By leading lines.

d) A combination of any of the above.

e) Repeating details such as tucks, gathers, button etc.

f) Unusual shapes and textures.

g) Applied design on a contrast background.

The placement of dark spots on a lighter colour background (or *vice versa* could emphasis the body part they are placed over. While enhancing the design by concentrating on a focal point the designer must bear in mind the figure and personality of the wearer.

Harmony: Harmony otherwise called unity. If the principle of proportion, balance, rhythm and emphasis are applied creatively, the resultant design is said to have the harmony. Unity means that all elements of the design work together to produce a successful visual effects. If anyone of the principles are not applied the resulting design will also lack harmony which means; if the principle of structural/decorative design with balanced proportion and quantitative and qualitative emphasis creating a rhythm of its own, give an outcome of harmony of unity. It is a result or an achievement which every designer should keep in mind while designing or drawing or arranging various elements or design for achieving/creating particular purpose of design.

Lack of application of any one principles of design, will result in a design which is not harmonious or not in harmony.

Proportion or Scale: Relationship in size between a part and the whole is defined to as proportion. For any design, an artist or a designer should aim for a sense of order of unity or oneness among the principles of design.

Proportion includes planning of the basic shape within a design. It may involve the scale of the forms within the design like diversion of space to create attractive space relationship where the variety of shapes, sizes and the general idea of unity of principles of designs are to be expressed. Optical illusion is created by changing partial arrangements to enhance the attractive portion that one wishes to enhance. e.g., puffed in the shoulders or increased width in sleeves etc.

Is the principles of design that involves a phasing relationships between all parts of a design with respect to each other. This may include:

- Planning of the basic shapes

- Division of spaces for a good relationship

Creating an optical illusion that will give an impression of proportion, when it is not possible to change the basic design.

Rhythm: Directs the movements of the eyes as one uses the details of a design. Therefore a rhythmic pattern needs to be established to give a costume unity.

There are no pe-requisite rules for establishing rhythm in a design. Rhythm is most effective when it is experienced in a quiet way.

It is the repeated use of lines or shapes to create pattern. Uniform rhythm is the repetition of the same space and is known as the order lines of rhythm. In progressive or graduated rhythm the size of the unit increases or decreases as it is repeated. Unequal rhythm is an unequal use of space and this rhythm is an unequal use of space and this is called as unorderliness of rhythm. In this type of rhythm the proportion are unbalanced; creating a larger space for enhancing the design and this finally calls in for expertise. This type of Rhythm gives thought provoking designs. The emphasis in such designs could be traced successfully by using unequal (or) unorderliness of rhythm. This reflects to a greater extract on the creativity of the designer and how an unequal division of space could bring out the best impact of the design with the emphasis shown within the design. Rhythm can be achieved through the combination of lines, shape, colour and texture by the following aspects in designing.

1) By regular repeats of trims, (button etc.) texture, and fabric design and prints.

2) Progression or radiation in sizes of trims, colours textures and fabric designs.

3) Radiation or movement from the central point occurring within structural details such as gathers, folds, tucks, darts etc.

4) Continuous flowing lines such as those in bonds of colours, textures and fabric designs.

Colour

CHAPTER 6

Colour is the most important element in fashion designing. Choosing colours is fun. But there is more to choosing an effective colour scheme and simply picking the colours that appeal to you just as there is more to being a connoisseur of fine art than knowing what you like. It is impossible to imagine a life without colours.

In colour as well as in music, harmony means an aesthetic arrangement of parts to form a pleasing whole; a musical composition, painting or a graphic design. All music from Mazart to Madonna consist of the same 12 notes and all graphic designs from Guttenburg to Glaser are the same palette of colours. Colours have to balance the harmony and rhythmic use in designing as done in music or fine art. If the science of colour harmony is knowing which colours to use, the art is knowing what order to put them in and what proportions of each. Following are a few points to help you along, the part to choosing a specific combination of two or more colours; a colour scheme, that you can use when you plan your fashion range, or fashion theme.

It is important to remember that the colour combinations used in your illustrations are on a very small scale, when used on a garment, it is magnified a hundred times. You will find that a seemingly innocuous colour suddenly look much bolder. In general, the larger the area, the bolder the colour appears, so it is often better to choose colour schemes with relatively weak tints and low contrast.

Colour is experienced both physically and psychologically when lighter waves strike the eyes in the absence of light, one does not experience colour, that is colour can be felt only in the presence of the light or white basic colour. Colours have an important role in drawing and in fashion designing as one of the greatest influencing element of designing and creating a design. They make a design attractive and lively. Various emotions and feelings can be expressed by colours. Following are some of the uses and emotions associated with familiar colours.

1 **Red:** Red is passionate, the colour of hearts and flames, it attracts our attention and actually speeds up the body's metabolism. For e.g., an Indian bride is always adorned in Red.

2 **Yellow:** is lively and happy, the colour of sunshine and flowers. Because it is so relentlessly cheerful, we find to fire of it quickly. e.g., yellow is exciting for day wear as well as evening wear, but it has the power of stabilising one's emotions since it signifies the advent of spring.

3 **Green:** Green is tranquil and pastoral, the colour of trees and grass. Bright green reminds us of spring and fertility-signifying life, but the other shades of green sometimes also become the colour of mildew, poison and jealousy. Some green such as olive green add sophistication to one's personality.

4 **Blue:** Blue is the colour of sky and sea. Light blue looks young and sporty but royal ordinary blue has a dignified wealthier.

5 **Purple:** Purple is the sophisticated colour, long associated with royalty. Purple is a highly fashionable colour usually to be used for formal evenings. It appears to be an artificial colour. So we find it hard to choose for our design. We do not often see it in nature, the lighter shades of purple have been choosen for women fashion in recent years.

6 **Brown:** Brown is rich and fertile like soil, and it is also sad and wistful like the leaves in winter. Brown if designed carefully appears to be quite romantic.

7 **White:** White is the colour of purity, virginity, innocence and peace, but is also associated with winter or the Christian bridal wear, over use of white can also be depressive.

8 **Black:** Black is the colour of night and death and often linked with evil. This is more orthodox approach to black. If used for evening or party wear it spells sheer elegance and wealth. It is also comfortable for winter.

Colour has three dimensions-they are hue, value and intensity.

Hue: is the actual colour of the colour wheel. We can say the other name of colour is hue.

Value: is the other face of hue, value refer to the lightness or darkness of colour.

Intensity: Refers to brightness and dullness of colour.

Colour Wheel

A Colour wheel or in other words chromatic circle is a very useful tool for differentiating colours and for establishing their relationship with each other. Colour wheel consist of 12 colours and the key colours of the colour wheel are primary colours, secondary colours and tertiary or intermediate colours. Red, Blue and Yellow are considered as primary colours and it cannot be obtained by mixing colours.

When two primary colours are mixed the secondary colours are obtained such as:

    Red   + Yellow = Orange

THE COLOUR WHEEL

— 1st Circle in the centre is the colour wheel

— 2nd Circle refers to the light colours (White + Hue of the colour wheel)

— 3rd Circle refers to the dull colours (Grey + Hue of the colour wheel)

— 4th Circle refers to the dark colours (Black + Hue of the colour wheel)

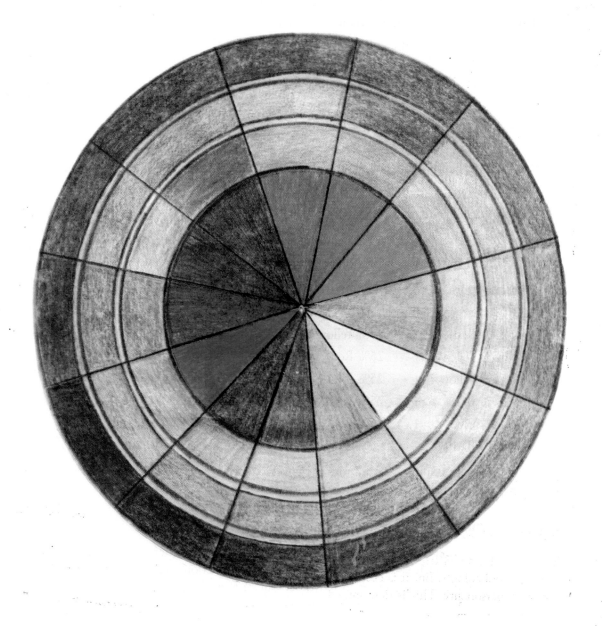

Yellow + Blue = Green and

Blue + Red = Violet

Orange, Green and Violet are secondary colours when a primary colour is intermixed with a secondary colour then obtained colours are called as tertiary or intermediate colours. They are:

Red + orange = Red orange.

Yellow + orange = Yellow orange.

Yellow + green = Yellow green.

Blue + green = Blue green.

Violet + Blue = Blue violet.

Red + Violet = Red violet.

The 12 colours of the colour wheel are Red, Red Orange, Orange, Yellow Orange, Yellow, Yellow Green, Green, Blue Green, Blue, Blue Violet, Violet, Red Violet.

Proportionate mixing of primary colours to achieve other colours needs the following percentages.

1) Primary colours: Red, Yellow, Blue.

2) Secondary colours:
   a) 50% Red + 50% Yellow = Orange.
   b) 50% Yellow + 50% Blue = Green.
   c) 50% Blue + 50% Red = Violet.

3) Tertiary/intermediate colours.
   a) 75% Red + 25% Yellow = Red Orange
   b) 75% Yellow + 25% Red = Yellow Orange
   c) 75% Yellow + 25% Blue = Yellow Green
   d) 75% Blue + 25% Yellow = Blue Green
   e) 75% Blue + 25% Red = Blue Violet
   f) 75% Red + 25% Blue = Red Violet

When white is added to a pure colour, tint of that colour is formed and when black is added to a pure colour then darker shades are formed.

Selecting Colours

Selection of colours depends largely on the personal selection whether a person likes to have warm or cool colours. But it is best to go for natural colour selection - meaning what exactly suits a certain personality. This is determined by the colour of hair, skin, eye and the bone structure.

The most important being skin as it is the largest important area. If a person is having the undertone of his/her skin colour similar to yellow, then the type of suitable colour is of warm colours. If the persons undertone of skin is without yellow and it is similar to blue, then the tone suitable is of cool colours. Hair and Eye colours are keyed by nature to skin tones.

The best way to learn which colour looks best on a person is to try them. Drape around the body in good visible light. Both natural and artificial, as different intensities of light make them appear quite different in these two situations, select the colour that appears most harmonious to the eye.

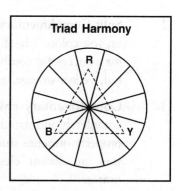

Triad Harmony

Using of Colours

1)   If a person is warm in colouring i.e., if their choice is blue, select a blue that has been modified by a warm colour such as yellow to give it a warm greenish blue to go with the person's natural colour.

2)   Eyes can be emphasised by wearing a make-up of a bit of the same colour but not brighter than the face. A brighter face tends to drain colour from the eyes.

3)   Colour and sheen are enhanced by contrasting colours or by the same colour.

4)   It is suggested that wearing a colour darker than skin is good unless you wish to emphasis its darkness or its sun tan.

5)   Dark skins with dark hair looks good in dark rich colours.

6)   If there is an excess of yellow in a person's skin, avoid using yellow, yellow-green and purple. Natural colour is emphasised by wearing a repetition of the colour or its compliment.

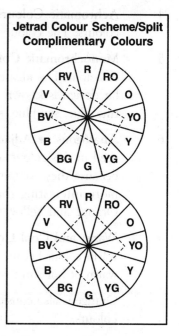

Jetrad Colour Scheme/Split Complimentary Colours

Colour Schemes

1   **The Triad Harmony:** This is the combination and three equidistant colours on the colour wheel, e.g., red, yellow, blue or orange, green, violet.

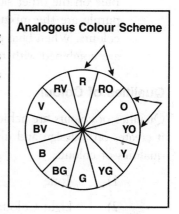

Analogous Colour Scheme

2   **Split Complimentary Colours:** This is the combination of four colours placed equidistant on the colour wheel. Their schematic arrangement needs some experience and practice for a successful combination. This is also known as Jetrad colour scheme e.g., blue violet, red, yellow orange, green, or blue violet, red violet, yellow orange, yellow green.

3   **Complimentary colours:** This are directly opposite on the colour wheel. They are completely unrelated in their normal   intensity. They show strong contrast. This property onriches thier quality. However strong and flashy complimentary colours appear, they are vibrant, elegant and sharp for e.g., yellow and purple, red and green, blue and orange.

4   **Achromatic Colours:** are literally "Colours without Colours" it is also called as neutral colours. The colour which comes under this colour scheme are black, white and grey.

5   **Monochromatic Colours:** One colour is used in various degrees of light and dark values of colour. The idea of using one colour with various values and intensities in a particular design is known as monochromatic colour scheme, e.g., blue, cobalt blue, ultramarine blue, sky blue, sea blue, navy blue etc.

6   **Analogous or Adjacent Colour Scheme:** Neighbouring colours of the colour wheel are used in this colour scheme. It is also known as similar colour scheme. They are related because they contain a colour in common. Due to this fact analogous colour scheme is more interesting than monochromatic colour scheme e.g., Red Orange and Orange, Orange and Yellow Orange etc.

7   **Warm and Cool Colours:** The primary colours such as red and yellow is considered as warm colour because of their effect upon us. This probably through our association with warm or hot sun rays and also the heat of fire and danger.

Orange is also considered as warm colour because it is obtained by mixing red and yellow colours.

Blue on the other side of colour wheel is considered as cool colour. Although green and purple are the mixture of cool and warm colours, they are generally classified as cool colours. When blue predominates, green and purple are more cool than when the colours are combined with red and yellow.

Qualities of Colour

Qualities of colours are achieved by combination of light or dark, the results are the effects that it creates on a design and ultimately to the personality of the wearer. Following are the different qualities of colours.

    1)   Tone

    2)   Light Colours

3)   Dull Colours

4)   Dark Colours

5)   Vivid Colours

1) **Tones:** Tone is formed by mixing white or black to the base colour. Tone is also regarded as an intensity of colour. For e.g., if dullness has to be achieved for a particular basic colour, grey (a combination of black and white in correct proportions) is added to it. This result in the degration of intensity of the basic colour and makes it more dull.

2) **Light Colours:** Addition of white to a basic colour results in the lighter shade of any colour. The hue is relatively important. Characteristics of light colours are soft ethereal. Light colours are popular among women's wardrobe, but it lacks eye grabbing quality that most designers seek, but a light colour can be effective in its own way and may actually stand out from the brash overconfident colour scheme that surrounds it.

3) **Dull Colours:** Addition of grey to a basic colour reduces the brightness, hence a dull colour is achieved. Dull colours are vague and diffuse, and create a blurry effect. However dull colours help reduce tension and can give colour scheme a meditative dream-like mood. Addition of more grey results in muddy shades.

4) **Dark Colours:** Combination of a primary base to the basic colours results in darker shade. Dark colours are often associated with royalty and have an aura of almost ponderous dignity for e.g., dark red, dark blue, dark purple, dark green etc. Black shade gives a feeling of heavy or adds weight to a design. Dark colours are often found in men's suits and formal wear. These colours are usually paired with lighter colours and are more conventional to use.

5) **Vivid Colours:** They are also called as surprising colours. The vivid or bright colours have powerful personality. They have a tendency to stand apart among other colours, but combination of two or more vivid colours is confusing. Vivid colour scheme is tricky, use of these colours is fine but they have a tendency for tiring eyes very quickly, e.g., fluorescent colours such as flourescent orange, lemon yellow, striking pink, electric blue and fluorescent green etc.

The Psychology of Clothing

CHAPTER 7

The wish to decorate or beautify the human body has been existed from the stone age when the early man painted his face and his body. Even though the beauty standards have changed, the desire remains constant.

The evolution of clothing has been closely interlinked with the factors such as social, economical and technological progress of each period in the history of man kind.

Basically what one sees and reacts is by their clothes. The clothes can determine the age of a person, his sex, nationality, occupation and his socio-economical conditions.

The clothes are also the symbol of the persons attitudes, values, interest, taste. By this we can easily study his or hers personal characteristics. They also fulfil important psychological needs of conformity and self-confidence.

As a person matures, he also grows his self-confidence and that individualistic nature will help him through selection of dresses from the range of choice in fabric, colours and designs according to the fashion trends.

Awareness of one's physical attributes and drawbacks as also awareness of one's personality is the essence of acquiring good clothing sense. Whether one is beautiful or not, it is possible to appear well-dressed and well-groomed by selecting clothes which brings out one's best features. The ability to select right clothing, colour, fabric and design and its matching accessories to suit the occasion indicates the person's good taste. There are some individuals who are born with the ability of selection where as others have to acquire them. Fashion designs are meant for model figures and can be adapted to suit one's own figure and personality.

Fabric is an integral part of dress making art and its proper selection is of utmost importance. It has to be selected to suit the personality of the wearer, the style of the dress, the occasion for which it has to be worn, for its fit and drape.

The quality of fabric depends on the type of the fibre, its inherent characteristics, its thickness the number of twists, the fabric constructions and finishes applied. The fibres can be natural or man made. Fabrics are got/manufactured in three types; 1 woven 2 knitted or 3 felted. Knitted fabrics are made with yarns looped together, using circular knitting machines, because these knitted fabrics are knitted with one single yarn it may frey easily even if a loop is cut or removed or opened.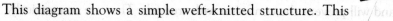

This diagram shows a simple weft-knitted structure. This term is used because the yarn is fed horizontally to form rows of loops in the next horizontal row.

This is the type of knitting which can be produced by hand using two knitting needles and a ball of yarn. Knitting machines can produce either a flat fabric or a tubular fabric according to type. The interlocked loops vertically is called wales and horizontal rows are called the courses. If the fabric is correctly on grain wales and courses intersect at 90°.

The stability of a simple knitted fabric is much less than that of ordinary woven fabric because any tension exerted on it will never be along with the line of a yarn, but will distort the loop structure, so that the fabric can be stretched in any direction. At one time hosiery and under-wear formed the main bulk of garments made from this type of fabric because shapes could be kept simple and the stretch of the knitted structure enabled a close fit to be obtained without complicated cutting or styling.

Knitted fabrics are now strenuously competing with woven fabrics in many clothing uses due to the fact that improved machines and techniques have produced. Knitted fabrics in complex structures which in some cases are equal to woven fabrics in stability and in addition manufactures and consumers are more accustomed to handling and using stretchable materials so that prejudice against knitted fabrics no longer exists to the extent to which it once did.

Techniques of fabric lamination and bonding, referred to us further course materials also serve to make knitted fabrics easier to handle by the designers and to give them more stability for garment use when required.

Knits are made of cotton, man-made fibres or their blends. They stretch more, do not crease easily and are ideal for sports and casual wear.

Felted fabrics are generally made of wool. These are made by pressing loose fibres together with heat and moisture.

Felt has been used by man for centuries and its manufacture is made possible by the fact that wool, and some other animal fibres, possess a natural tendency to felt or mat together under the influence of heat, moisture and mechanical pressure. In this way, webs of wool fibres can be consolidated into a fabric. A fabric produced in this way is entirely without grain because the flat webs of fibres are non-directional, be the fibres point in all directions felt can be cut in any direction without trying or unravelling because of the compact fibre arrangement. Unfortunately this convenience is marred by distinct deficiencies in drape, stability so that felt is of very little use for normal garment making.

If felt is to be strong and stable the fibres must be consolidated that the material is still and heavy with very little draping property. If felt is made soft and supple its properties of tensile strength, resistance to abrasion and distortion are too low to be of practical value for normal garment interlinings. Certain types of woven and knitted fabrics are also given felted finish which gives them the appearance of felt in that no yarn structure is apparent and the fabric appears to be composed entirely of fibres. However, closer examination, tearing and cutting the fabric will show the basic yarn structure and will prevent the confusion with true felt. They are economically attractive. The conditions of the second world war promoted the Germans to produce non-wovens as cheap and substitute materials which has its own character and properties. Initially the producers were unsure of its direction, they tried short life garments like underwears and knickers but the manufacturing cost was too high therefore they have developed these non-wovens for interlining for clothing and industrial fabrics for protective clothing in hospitals and factories, resulting in the production of filter fabrics, face masks, airline head-rest covers, sheets, table cloths, overalls, medical materials and household cleaning cloth which is now well established. Recently non-wovens are also used by armed services, made to NATO specifications, provide 24 hrs protection against chemical attack involving toxic gases and liquids, also available with flame retardant finish.

The most commonly used fibres used for non-wovens are nylon, polyester and viscose. These are different methods used for the formation of web and variety of ways in which the fibres are compacted and held together to become a non-woven fabric. It is made in 100% synthetic fibres which have been hear bonded by sophisticated methods.

The fabric which is most commonly used are the woven fabrics. The fibres are first converted into yarns which can be fine or coarse, tightly or loosely twisted, smooth or rough. The warp or lengthwise yarn are stronger and are held taut on the loom. The weft or crosswise yarns are then used to interlace or weave the fabric. The closely woven edge of the fabric are called the selvedge. It gives additional firmness to the fabric. As the weave of the warp and weft yarns are closer the count will be higher and fabric will be finer. The loosely woven fabric is coarse and has less number of yarns per square inch.

The warp yarns are parallel to the selvedge and weft yarns are at right angles to the warp.

When the warp and weft are interlaced exactly at 90° angle then fabric grain to perfect and is called as grained fabric. It is very essential for good sewing as it affects the fall or drape of the garment.

Fabric is woven in different types of weaves such as Dobby, Jacquard, Satin, Twill etc. to get various textures. It is the textures which affects both tactile and visual quality of fabrics.

The visual quality are its roughness and smoothness of the fabric, its shine or dullness depends upon, the amount of light reflected by the fabric such as smooth fabric will reflect more light and shines up when compared to the coarse fabric.

Its tactile quality means the feel of touch of the fabric which we check with our finish while purchasing the fabric. The tactile quality can be referred to check the stiff or silky quality of fabric. Most of people believe in tactile quality of testing than the visual.

We select the fabric according to the seasons because of the properties of fabric as one would wear cottons for summer because it is light and more absorbent. Wool and silk for the winter because it gives warmth because of its thickness and its natural insulating property. Synthetic fabrics dry quickly and easily and does not go limp in the damp weather. So one will select this for the rainy or the monsoon season.

Fabrics can have psychological effects on the wearer. People will be fresh in organdie and crisp in cotton, very delicate and feminine in chiffons, dignified in silk and rustic in handlooms. After the cloth is woven, it is dyed, printed and chemically treated to improve the finish of the fabric and for good look of the texture, colour and its performance.

Some of the most common finishes are sanforizing, mercerizing and wash-n-wear. Where sanforizing means to pre-shrink the fabric such as polyester and other synthetic fabrics. Mercerizing means strengthening the fabric and to improve or give lusture to the fabric.

Wash-n-wear which means this is the finish which is given to make the fabric crease-resistant. Some fabric are made up of different fibres and this type of mixing different fibres to construct a fabric are called as blending. It is done to improve the quality of fabric and to reduce its cost. Cotton and silk are blended to make the fabric stronger and less expensive than pure silk. It has lusture and also attractive and durable. In terricotton fabric polyester and cottons are blended. This fabric has the absorption quality of cottons and crease resistant quality of polyester and more comfortable to wear and easy to care of.

There are many varieties of fabrics available in market and it is important to know about the basic properties of fabric so that it is easier to choose the type of fabric needed and judging its quality or it is best to look at the label details.

One should also know how many percentage of blends are made in the fabric so that you can make out how it will react with. For example, in terricotton fabric more percentage of cotton and less percentage of polyester is blended for less expensive but it will be easily creased to form wrinkles but comfortable to wear.

One should know the psychology of clothing, so that one who know how selection of fabric is made to suit the person, his dress styles and to suit the occasion.

Selection should be made in such a way that it matches his figure. Silk, chiffon and crape fabric drapes well and falls into gentle folds to give a feminine look, so it can be used for womens who wants to look delicate.

There are fabric which adds bulk to the body such as brushed cottons, velvette and other heavy fabrics. They tend the person look more heavy. It will suit the thin and tall person who wishes to look bulky.

People who are thin should wear fabric which are more shiny and lustrous because they reflect light and emphasis the body contours. Dull texture do absorb light but do not enlarge the size of the body.

Occasion: Basically the dresses which are worn at evening or night should be made in dark colours and shiny fabrics.

Dull and light colour will go well for day-to-day wearing.

Knitted fabrics are ideal for sports and casual wear.

One should choose to make garments from the fabric which are comfortable to wear for a longer period of time and fashionable garment should be selected to wear for any short occasions.

It is also important to know to select fabric for the particular styled outfit.

One should select fabric which are stiff for the outfits which stands well and which needs stiffness and less fall and drape where as the same which is selected to make an aline skirt in stiff fabric cannot be used for stitching a circular skirt because it needs more falling material such as chiffon and crape.

There are different types of style in the silhouette and the designer should know to select the proper type of fabric which will suit the design.

If the firmly woven fabric gives a crisp and stiff effect. Knitted fabric give more ease and comfortable but cling to the body shape and do not drape like other fabric such as chiffon and china silk. Knitted fabric needs careful handling because they stretch easily so the design of the garment should be simple and should have minimum scams and should be cut with enough ease added to avoid the cling.

The stiff fabrics which looks crisp will not cling to the body so it can cover the irregularity of the figure.

Designer should see to that they select a plain weaved fabric outfit to be stitched with extra trimmings where as if the fabric has some different weave the importance should be given to emphasis the weaves and reduce the use of trimming as the weave itself can enhance the beauty of the outfit.

Some Traditional Textiles of India

CHAPTER 8

The India of today succeeded to a rich heritage in Architecture, Music and other Fine Arts and Crafts, which for scores centuries had been steadily growing despite the rise and fall in the destinies of its people.

Aliens who came, whether as traders or as invaders, ended with the solitary exception of the English by making India their home and by getting absorbed in its original inhabitants. The intermingling of races did start new currents and cross currents in the flow of our culture, but it made our culture richer and fuller.

The culture, which India invariably shared with its neighbours and others, by earning for itself an honoured place -second to none- amongst the nations of the world. Its fame spread to lands far and near, even in those remote ages of which no written historical record exists. Whilst the missionary zeal our religious emissareees carried the spiritual aspects of our culture to the distant corners of the globe, the spread of our culture to the distant corners of the globe, the spread of our culture on its temporal side was entirely due to our traders and exporters who were our cultural ambassadors abroad. Through the export of its famous textiles, the exquisite beauty and finesse which was almost legendary, ancient and medieval India attained an unrivalled position in the international textile trade, which she maintained till not-so very-long ago. According to George Birdwood, India "was probably the first of all countries that perfected weaving and the art of its gold brocades and filmy muslins". Can it be wondered then that the textile products of the Indian craftsmen were eagerly and even anxiously looked for and awaited in the markets of the world ? How could competitors ever hope to catch up with a country that was thousands of years ahead of them in this art? They only ban the use of the Indian fabrics within their own country. The Roman Senate was probably the first to pass a law (about 600 A.D.) prohibiting the wearing of the Indian silk garments by men. A little more than a century ago England prohibited by law the use of the Indian calico. This was the beginning of the two-centuries-long unremitting war against India's supremacy in textiles.

As is only natural, a crop of legends have collected around the finesse and the delicacy of the fabrics which the Indian weavers produced with the aid of little more than their human hands. One such, which is widely believed to be authentic, might be related here. The austere Mughal Emperor Aurangazeb chided his gifted daughter Zebunnisa, for not being properly dressed because her body could be seen through. "But I have no less than seven suits on" protested the lady "One on top of another". "Put on some more" commanded Emperor "to obscure the transparency".

As in Architecture, Music and other Fine Arts, India has its own distinctive contribution in the production of textiles so far as artistic designs, harmonious and beautiful colour schemes and, of course, the finesse of fabrics are concerned. Hand spinning and weaving though carried on a small scale and developed slowly as cottage industry had already reached a high stage of perfection, even as early as 327 B.C. We catch glimpses of it in the descriptions, sent home by Alexander's soldiers, of costumes worn by the people of India. Foreign visitors to this country, on their departure, always carried away with them priceless treasure, pieces of silk, brocades and muslins. Cargo's laden with our wondrous fabrics, were invariably welcomed by other countries. This marvelous technique of the craft which has raised it to the status of a 'Fine Art' has developed through hundreds of generations of craftsmen who formed an exclusive class or guild and handed down from father to son, the knowledge gained and the progress made so that each successive generation of craftsmen added something to it and became more and more efficient, producing better results. Another characteristic of traditional Indian textiles common to all artistic creation of human hands is that, each piece bears the stamp of the individuality of the craftsman who produced it. Thus, it has a human imprint of its own. As the gifted writer Shm. Kamal Dongerkery has said the traditional textiles of India "reveal the background of rich culture. They give artistic shape and form to the ideas and ideals which inspire the lives of the people" and thus provide one of the most reliable hallmark of the cultural development of the people.

The craft was carried on in the villages of some of the important provinces of India, especially around the coastal towns and cities. It was not restricted, as a profession, to men alone, but women too, in their own leisure hours, helped their men in spinning and weaving and thus, added to the family income. Indeed, in certain provinces like Assam, tradition required women to achieve some degree of skill in the arts of weaving and spinning and even today unmarried girls in Assam are not considered quite eligible for matrimony, unless they have acquired some grounding in this useful art. But the craft flourished mostly as a result of the patronage extended to it by the royalty and aristocracy, which played a vital role in its development.

To suit the tastes of the royal and noble families, the standard of production had to be very high and ever progressive.

Different types and varieties of textiles were produced in different parts of India and thus we hear of Banaras and Surat Brocades, Dacca Muslins, Cashmere Shawls, Gujarat Patolas. In the following pages, an attempt has been made to present, in bare outlines, the chief characteristics of some of the outstanding traditional textiles of India. Illustration of several of these fabrics have been added to their descriptions.

It would perhaps interest our readers to learn that in a number of ancient families are cherished, even today, as valuable heirlooms, some beautiful specimens of our traditional textiles. A good few of these have been presented to some national museums which proclaim to the nation and the world, of Fine Arts and the glory that was India".

Muslins

Dacca(now the capital Bangladesh) was, for centuries, synonymous with the finest Muslins the world has ever produced by hand or machine. In the words of Dr. Forbes Wastson "with all our machinery and wondrous appliances we have been hitherto unable to produce a fabric which for its fineness and utility can equal the 'woven air of Dacca'. Indeed, the Dacca weavers magic hands produced such exquisitely fine and delicate fabrics that the poetic names 'abi-rawan' (Flowing water), 'Bafta-Hawa' (Woven-air), 'Shabnam' (Evening dew) were justifiably given to them. Exhibits in some of our museums prove even today that a yard's width of the Muslin could easily pass through a lady's ring. Then there are legends which have collected around these fabrics. One of them relates that a five yard piece of the Muslin could be packed in a match box. It is however, an authenticated fact that a 15 yard piece of 36 inches width 'Mulmal Khas' (Royal Muslin) in the reign of the Emperor Jehangir, weighed only 900 grams. Of course 'Mulmal Khas' was the Dacca Muslin.

The value of Dacca Muslins is estimated by the number of warp threads in a given length of the material as compared with its weight. The greater the length and the number of the threads, with comparatively less weight, the higher would be the price. For instance a yard's width of 'Mulmal Khas' the finest Muslin, was known to have 1000 to 1800 threads in the warp, and the weaver took five months to weave 10 yards of fabric. The weaving of these fabrics could only be done during the rainy season, because for the weaving of such an extremely fine fabric, a humid atmosphere was essential.

Dacca Sarees

Up to the beginning of the 19th century, the Dacca Muslin sarees, one of the most artistic and beautiful specimens of handloom textiles, were counted amongst their valuable and cherished possessions by the women of Bengal. Even today, these sarees are beautiful in their design, but alas the art of making fine Muslins is no more, and sarees too are not half as fine as they were in the past.

The sarees are generally gray, white or black with blue or black designs. Occasionally, the patterns are woven in bright coloured cotton, or silver or gold threads. The Dacca Muslins with the woven-in pattern are known as 'Jamdani' and the typical designs of flowers or figures used by the Dacca weavers are known as "Jamdani" pattern. The sarees have very bold and large Jamdani pattern on "Anchal" "Palloos" (end portion) and the borders. The rest of the saree is generally covered with numerous small bootties. The common motif is the round design bootties, which suggest Chameli (Jasmine) flowers and around these are sprays of flowers spread all over the *saree* called a "Bottedar" *saree*, and when the sprays are grouped in diagonal lines, the saree is known as 'Terchha'. But when the floral design forms a network which covers the entire field, then the pattern is known as "Jatar".

Some in Jamdani designing, the flowers are clustered together like the settings of jewels, and then the pattern is given the poetic name of 'Panna Hazare' (thousand emeralds). If a running floral pattern covers the whole field, the expression Phulwar is used, but if the flowers are large and life size the Jamdani is called Toredar.

The borders and Palloos or Anchal (end portion) of *sarees* are generally decorated with distinctive figure designs. The figures chosen represent birds, animals, and human beings. Peacock or 'mayura' and herons or 'hansa' seem to be popular as bird-figures in the designs of Dacca sarees. Also some of the motifs indicate the influence of mythological legends, as well as of the local traditions. The designs are commonly accepted as of Persian origin but many of the designs depict incidents from the Hindu mythology also.

The most striking feature of the Jamdani pattern is the skill of the weaver in being able to depict the conception of actual motion in the figures he weaves in. Many a design presents birds with flapping wings as if they are about to fly away. The outline of figures are always bold, straight and invariably geometric in clear cut lines. Also the intervening space is so well balanced with lines and flowers that a most delightful effect is produced by the combination. It may well be imagined that the weaving of such masterpieces called for the highest skill and craftsmanship with almost unlimited patience as each design must have involved months of work.

An idea of the weavers may be formed from the following description in the process of weaving.

Chanderi Sarees

The Muslins woven in Chanderi, a place near Gwalior, have earned a name for themselves because of their fine quality. Chanderi sarees are mostly cotton with borders and palloos woven in silk or gold threads. Sometimes mixed threads of silk and cotton are used for weaving the fabrics known as 'Garbhreshmi'. The palloos of these are very artistically ornamented with gold threads while the ground of the saree is checked, with booties in the centre of each check-square. The borders are woven with double threads which produce an effect of two colours, one on each side. The *sarees* are woven in nine-yard lengths and are very much valued by the Maharashtrian ladies.

Baluchar Buttedar

Baluchar, a small town near Marshidabad, has become a noted and a highly valued name in the handloom textile history of India. The artisans of the locality produced very artistic figured silk sarees known as Baluchar Buttedar. In Baluchar Buttedar, as in Dacca sarees, the Palloos were the most elaborately ornamented portions. The field of the remaining portion of the saree was decorated with small booties of some floral design or figure design of birds. The special feature of

Baluchar Buttedar is that the design used for the ornamentation show a strong influence of Mughal Art, which is famous for its portraits. The weaver of Baluchar chooses motifs of human figures and the popular 'Toranj' (also called 'Kalka' or 'Guldasta') which is the most popular motif in weaving, embroidery and printing throughout India under its present application the mango design. In the design of the palloo, the famous ever popular 'Toranj' are seen as though these are set in a frame. The border of the frame is again elaborately decorated with pictorial representation of a lady smelling a flower and seated. The interspaces are filed with neatly arranged rows of 'Toranj' lined with an outer border of flowering plant. The border design which is a simple and straight combination of a small toranj and flowering plant is continued for the borders of the whole saree.

The subjects for portraits were either a lady or a noble man dressed in Persian dress and holding a flower or riding a horse or smoking. Though the subjects were always of Islamic origin, yet the Baluchar Buttedar were very popular amongst the Hindu ladies. This gesture indicates a complete absence of intolerance existing between the two communities.

Later on, probably due to the desire for the patronage of the English bosses of the East India Company the woven-in-pictorial subjects came to include figures dressed in European clothes, holding instead of the traditional flower, a wine glass.

The wonderful art of weaving figured fabrics in Baluchar is lost for ever and a few extinct-scattered specimen in some museums are the sad mementos of the perfection it has achieved.

Kam Khwab, Bafra and Ab-i-Rawan (Brocade)

Kam Khwab is the name given to red gold brocades. Brocades is the expression used by Westerners who at first called it 'Kin Kab' or 'Cin Con'. According to their conception, brocades are thick textiles with woven-in pattern very prominently thrown up on the surface of the cloth. Consequently, not only Kam Khwabs, but other similar textiles also like buftas as Amrus, and Himrus are known to them by the comprehensive English name 'brocades'. The poetic name Kam Khwab expresses the dream like beauty and richness of the fabric. It literally means only a little less (Kam) than a dream (Khwab) for a dream (Khwab) reduced (Kam) to reality.

The real Kam Khwabs are woven with pure gold threads and the silk yarn is added to provide a body and as a means for colour illuminations. Silver or gold plated silver threads are also used for keeping down the price but gold is usual. These are heavy fabrics and are generally used for making palloos, blouses and for men's half-sleeve Indian Jackets, long-coats (Angarkhas or Achkans), ceremonial robes (chogas) and also later on came to be used for curtains and for upholstering the furniture of Public Rooms and Durbar Halls of Princess.

Bafta or Pot Thans

These are the brocades in which the major portion of the fabric is closely woven silk with patterns in gold or silver at regular intervals. This is not is heavy or thick as Kam Khwabs but is heavier than the other textiles. Baftas are also used for blouses and Indian skirts (Lehengas or Damnas) and for men Angarkhas or Ackhans too.

Ab-i-Rawans

These are silk gauze materials with gold or silver patterns only on certain portions. Silk gauze series with women-in gold border and palloos, are called Ab-i-rawans. The literal meaning of this poetic name is 'flowing water'.

Although brocades are a speciality of Banaras for which it is famous yet these are also manufactured at Surat and at Ahmedabad and depict the traditional floral motif. In old brocades, motifs representing animals and human figures enclosed with borders are in use.

Himrus and Amrus

Himrus are the famous silk brocades of Hyderabad (Deccan). The State's second largest town Aurangabad is the chief centre of the art of Himru weaving. Himru probably a derivative of the Sanskrit Him (snow) is fabric used in winter. The ground is Cotton and Silk is used for the brocade on the surface. The yarn used for weaving Himrus is spun so as to produce, when woven, the effect of a warm soft material like wool. The peculiarity of the Himru is that the silk thread which is used to form a pattern of the surface of the cloth, is carried to the reverse side of the cloth and is collected there in clumsy long loops. This forms a rather loose but soft warm layer. Further the accumulation of loose threads on the reverse of the cloth, necessitates a lining to all garments made of Himru cloth. Thus Himru garments make very warm clothing suitable for the cold season.

When silk thread is used exclusively for weaving Himru, the fabric is called 'Amru'. Amru are generally made in Ahmedabad, Surat and Banaras. Himrus are used for men's Achkans, Chogas, and for female wear also, e.g., for blouses and Lehangas, for generations, the Nawabs of Surat used a special quality of Himru fabrics for their dresses which was called the 'Nawab's Himru'. These fabrics are also used for upholstery and curtains.

Paithan and Pitamber

Paithanis are the beautiful and rich sarees made at Pattan or Paithan in the state of Hyderabad (Deccan). These are exquisitely fine silk fabrics with gauze like texture ornamented with gold patterns woven in the texture of the colour. The borders and the palloos which are woven separately as gold brocades are sewed on the saree. The colour of the saree is usually dark orange red or yellow with gold lines arranged in checks or stripes. The interspaces are usually filled in with a figure design depicting a goose with an olive branch in its beak.

The borders and the palloos have very striking designs in bright and showy colours such as moss-green, canary yellow, and bright pink. The common motif of the design is the peacock supporting a big vase with sprays of brilliantly coloured flowers so arranged as to form a Persian cone pattern.

The Paithani palloo does not have the favourite peacock in the design, but it depicts the harmonious arrangement of the sprays and the surrounding floral design. The vase with sprays is placed between two pillars joined with the toran (arch). The design is worked in silks of blue, red, and white colours on a field of pure translucent gold. The whole effect is gorgeous and is eminently artistic in its perfect harmony.

In olden days Paithanis were usually woven to order for the Royal family and the weaver took months to complete a single piece. The value of genuine real Paithani ranged between Rs. 2000 to Rs. 3000. In modern times, however, such highly valued and gorgeous Paithanis are not woven.

Pitambars are bright coloured silks 5 yards in length with gold border sewn on them. These are worn by men specially when performing any of the religious rituals.

Patola : It is an artistically ornamented fabric. It is a specimen of wonderful combination of the craft of tie-dying (Bandhana) and weaving. Patola is mostly in use as a wedding saree in Kathiawar and Gujarat. In Java and in Indonesia too the Patola fabric is used for wedding dresses. The fabric is so exquisitely and so highly valued that it is handed down from generation to generation in the family. Women of Gujarat and Kathiawar treasure the possession of patola with pardonable pride.

Patola unlike the other ornamented fabrics, is invariably woven in just the plain weave. The elaborate and intricate patterns which mark the Patola sarees are produced by the wonderful art of Bandhana or tie-dying. The silk yarn with which Patolas are woven, is first dyed by the Bandhana process before it is put on the loom. The yarns, both warp and weft, are dyed in the lightest of colours. Then they are stretched on the ground, and the dyer proceeds to mark certain portions to indicate the lines of the desired design. Weavers wife who helps him in his work, then ties up the marked portions with cotton thread so tightly that the next dye can't penetrate through to the tied up portions. The yarn is then immersed in dye-baths of the desired colours and shades. The operation of tie-and dye is repeated several times until all the colours and shades required for the planned design have been applied to the yarn. The dyer begins with a light colour, passes next to a bright one and applies the dark colour at the very last. Then the weaver starts on his job. The warp threads are arranged in pre-arranged sequence, and the weft is then interlaced one by one very carefully to form the planned design. The process of producing a Patola, is therefore a very laborious one and is extremely complicated too. Meticulous care and a good deal of creative imagination is needed for making the correct portions on yarns for dyeing in different colours of the patterrn. A very retentive memory is another essential requisite for registering and recalling accurately the sequence of the coloured threads in the pattern. Thus only a few traditional designs are used for Patola patterns. The following eight designs are used by the weavers of Pattan as described by Mr. G.V. Patel.

1) Nari-junjar bhat or dancing girl and an elephant design. It has necessareely a parrot included in it.

2) Pan bhat or leaf design. It is said to be the leaf of the sacred pipal tree (Ficus Religion).

3) Rattan chawak bhat or the cross of diamonds design. It has inter-spread diamonds also.

4) Okhar bhat or water crest design. The real name of this design on investigation at Pattan, appears to akhort bhat, i.e., the walnut design.

5) Phulvadi bhat or floral design, is generally enclosed in diapers out-lined by a single line. Each diaper contains three flowers.

6) Wagh-Kunjar bhat or tiger-elephant design. The animals alternate with each other in the design.

7) Chabri bhat or basket design. Here each enclosure containing an elephant is made up of four quadrants which look as if forming a basket when two of them are taken together.

8) Chowkhadi bhat or a diaper with a double outline design. Each diaper included three flowers borne on a stem.

There is one more design which is used for dhoties (the loin cloth worn by men). This design consists of the Devnagri alphabet and the forms of the letters follow those of the mantras (hymns) in religious books.

Pattan, a place in Kathiawar, is reputed to be the birth-place of Patola. The weavers of Pattan later migrated to Bombay, Ahmedabad and Surat and the making of Patolas started at these places also.

Orissa weavers also have adopted the Patola technique for weaving their special fabrics like curtains, bed spreads, *odhnis*, (scarfs worn over the head and draped round the shoulders and waist by women) and sarees. The famous Sambalpore sarees are woven like Patolas.

Bandhanis

Bandhanis or Choonaris are the colourful sarees and *odhnis* dyed by tie-and dye process. These are popular amongst the women of Gujarat, Kathiawar, Rajputana and Sindh, Premalata Jayakar in her article on Tie Dyed Fabrics of India', in "Marg" refers to Bandhanis in the following words- "It is an auspicious garment. A symbol of youth and romance, love play and 'Suhag' (wifehood) of Hindu women. It is a garment of laughter".

Indian women are known for their love for bright colours. Also the tradition and the customs of wearing special colours on different festivals makes it necessary for them to become familiar with the art of dying at home. Thus besides the expert professional dyers every Indian girl learns by practice a good deal of the art of dying and Bandhani work.

Bandhanis differ from Patola in regard to the stage at which they are dyed. Like Patolas they are dyed by the tie-and-dye process, which however, is done after the fabric is woven. The fabric is folded over several times until it is reduced to a small thick square or a rectangular piece. The piece is then damped and pressed on a block on which a design has been carved. The impressed portions are picked up by the finger nails (the nails are allowed to grow specially for this purpose and are used as a sort of pincers) and are then tied up with cotton thread in a thickness sufficient to resist the dye. It needs training and great skill to pick up all the layers at once and make it crinkle in a particular given manner.

The Bandhanari, or the woman who does the tieing up work, works swiftly ties up all the impressed portions without cutting the thread but carries it over from one point to the next. The dyeing process is carried out in the same order as in Patolas, starting with the light colours and finishing with the dark ones. But each time, before a new shade or colour is applied the tieing up process has got to be repeated.

Usually, the designs used are copies of a few traditional ones and by the practice of tieing-up the same design over and over again the Bandhanaris become experts to such an extent that they are able to dispense with the process of impressing the fabric with the design.

The motif of the traditional designs used for Bandhanis represents animals, birds, flowers and dancing dolls. When elaborate designs are used the Bandhanis are known as 'Gharchola'. In some of the expensive 'Gharchola' gold threads are woven in to form checks or squares, and then the designs are formed in each of the squares by the tie-and-dye process. The 'Choonaries' are very light fabrics, and the design for these consist of dots or pin heads irregularly spread all over the field of the cloth. Sometimes the dots are grouped together to form a design, and the design is known as 'Ek bundi' (one dot), 'Char bundi' (four dots) and 'Sath bundi' (seven dots).

It might interest our readers to know that in some parts of Rajputana, e.g., Alwar, professional dyers existed till a couple of decades ago, who could dye even the finest Muslin into different colours, one on each side of the fabric at the modest charge of only annas four a yard. This art too is now extinct but specimens can be found in some museums.

Kalmendar of Kalamdar

This is the name given to the hand painted cotton fabrics. They are so called because the artist works out the designs on the material with a fine steel brush not unlike a pen (Kalam). The process is very much the same as used for Batik work. The basic principle, namely resist dyeing, being common to both. The material is first dyed in pale pink and then stretched out tight. The artist then traces the outline of the design with his Kalam or fine steel brush dipped in melted wax. The fabric is then dyed deep red and finally washed in hot water to melt away the wax. This produces the design in pale pink on the background of deep red.

Kalamdar fabrics are also called Palampores in the textile trade. They are available in rectangular pieces and are popular with Hindus and Muslims alike, the former use them as canopies for the images of their Gods and the latter as praying carpets. Those designed for Hindus portray scenes from the Hindu origin. The latter depicts the conventional Mirhab with panels forming a frame enclosing the 'Persian Tree of Life' complete with birds and the branches and animals resting under its shade. The craftsmanship and the skill of the dyer is amply borne out by the excellent portrayal of the minutest details with amazing accuracy. The French traveller Bernier who visited

India in 1663, during the reign of Emperor Shahjehan, thus describes the fabric which formed the drippings of the Imperial courtyard - "And lined within with those chittes. Or cloth painted by a pencil of Masulipatam, purposely brought and contrived with such vivid colour and flowers, so naturally drawn, of a hundred several fashions and shapes, that one would have said it was a hanging parterre".

KORA SILK

Kora silk or silk cotton *saree* of Tamil Nadu.

The tussar like texture of these *sarees* silk yarn is due to the raw untreated silk yarn that is used to weave them. The same silk when boiled and treated with chemicals is used in pure silk *sarees* and lend them a much softer and finer texture.

In silk cotton *sarees*, the silk thread is used in the warp and gas merserised fine 100 count cotton yarn is used in the weft.

In pure Kora silk *sarees*, the silk thread is used both in warp and weft. Synthetic or tested *zari* as it is called with 10% silk silver content is used to decorate the pallu and borders of these *sarees*. The design and motifs used to decorate the body and pallu are the traditional designs that are also used in the Negamam cotton *sarees* and Kanchipurm silk *sarees*.

The fibre silk *saree* has a characteristically narrow bordered with a rich pallu decorated with motif which are often repeated in the body of the saree. The traditional design includes stylized peacock, swan, parrot, elephants, mangoes and paisley motif. The geometric patterns are also used.

Sarees are priced between Rs. 600 to Rs. 2,000. It depends whether they are woven with Kora silk and cotton yarns or only Kora silk yarn and also the intricacy and richness of the design.

Brocades of tissue *saree* are also woven with silk yarn on warp and saree thread on the weft with intricate *zari* pattern on the pallu. These *sarees* cost Rs. 3,000 to Rs. 5,000 and each *saree* comes with matching blouse piece woven along side which lends the special attraction.

Mostly deep traditional colours are used like vermillion red, deep green, golden yellow, peacock blue, deep magenta, black and navy blue. But now lighter colour like cream white, sky blue, lemon yellow, pale pink, lavender are also being introduced to cater to the taste of younger college going and working women.

Yarn: The silk yarn of the *saree* comes from Bangalore and cotton yarn from Coimbatore (the Manchester of South). Both the yarns are dyed in the local dying unit with chemical dyes, the half fine *zari* as it is called, comes from Surat. The weaver takes three to five days to weave a *saree*.

BANDANI

Infinite variety of designing can be created by combining traditional art from remote corners of Gujarat and Rajasthan.

Tie dyeing is a resist dyeing process. Certain portions are tied to create the design as tying resists the penetration of dye. In India dying has been carried out for centuries. This popular craft flourished during the Mughal period and during British Empire. It can be used to pattern big and small articles of personal clothing and for household furnishing. A variety of patterns can be created and no two designs are ever exactly alike. The manner in which certain area of fabric are protected from dye produces the specific pattern.

Designing can be created by usual method like knotting, binding, pleating and twisting, folding, tying and stitching. New patterns give life to expressing innate aesthetic urge born out of traditional art. Designing can take new direction when these traditional art can be commercialized in different ways.

Abroad you can find two or three types of basic dresses. Frock, Gown, Trouser and Shirts. In this way India is very rich in costumes and accessories. Each and every state has its own design, which is entirely different from its neighbouring states. Punjabi dress, saree, blouse, ghagara *choli*, Nehru Shirt and *pajama, lungi, dhothi* etc. Again a designer has lots of themes to design with, take *choli* for instance Rajasthan and Gypsy, *choli* with back open and with patch and quilting work, to suit the desert climate, Marathi's short front knotted *choli*, with bead work or of Irkal border, Coorgi's long sleeve cut on bias grain with V-neck, Madrasi patti blouse. The Bengali woman has won the race in this field. They have five varieties of blouses, with lots of trim frill, piping with half sleeve, one fourth sleeve, puff sleeve, 3/4 sleeve with lace or fancy ruffles attached.

Another item is *gaghara-choli*. Mysorean *gaghara* is attached with plain body which is hidden by top tight fitting long blouse and half sleeve. Rajasthani's colourful satin or cotton *lloulahga* with hip length blouse, loose fitting. Madrasi wears, gathered or pleated *lehanga* with *saree* blouse and half *saree*.

Embroidered fabrics

India is rich in embroidered fabrics. The Indian art of embroidery is an ancient one. Its origin can be traced right back to the Vedic age and it appears to have been well-developed by the time of the great epics. Later on, the influence of incoming races and tribes particularly those which migrated from the hills contributed a great deal towards the development of the art along the lines which have given it the present form. "The stitches employed and art conceptions displayed" by these early artists indicate the extent of their knowledge of the art. It may be noted that throughout the mountains and valleys of India, the art is very popular and is assiduously pursued by men and women. The very colourful embroidery produced is not always intended only for the market, but also for home use as well.

A few of the better-known embroidered fabrics may now be briefly described.

The Punjabi Phulkari

Phulkari really means flower (Phul) work (Kari). These were the conventional ceremonial shawls worn by the Hindu bride at her wedding when going round the sacred fire with the bridegroom.

It is a popular saying in Punjab that when the girl is born in a family the mother, or may be the grand-mother, starts embroidering a Phulkari to be presented to the girl on her wedding day.

The women of the Jat community are specialised in Phulkari work. In almost all the districts of the Punjab, wherever this community has settled down the Phulkari work has originated and flourished. The peasant women of Tohtak, Hissar, Gurgaon and Karnal are known for embroidering the best Phulkaries. Rohtak is considered to be the home of Phulkari work.

The stitch for Phulkari embroidery is the simple darn stitch. The material on which the embroidery is done is rough Khaddar, but the thread used for the embroidery is silk and the colours used are white, red, yellow or green. The colour of the Khaddar material is invariably red, maroon or brown.

The Phulkari motifs generally are of floral patterns, but geometric patterns are also used. For instance in the Bagh or Shalimar design, the entire material is covered with a geometric pattern. In orthodox Phulkari, however, the same floral pattern is embroidered only at intervals on the cloth, intervening portions of which are left plain. Sometimes, only the borders are embroidered to a width of 3 to 4 inches and the centre of the material is left plain. This pattern is known as Chobes.

The choice of the design is wide, but very often they appear to be almost identical because of the close and compact stitches used. It is remarkable that the illiterate village women choose designs and the colour schemes which have a charm and beauty of their own and which are worked out unerringly by memory.

Shishedar Phulkaries

These are different from the other Phulkaries. The special feature is that the embroidery is embellished with tiny mica or looking glass (Shisha) discs fixed to the cloth by botton-hole stitches. The material embroidered in this way is very often silk, or even satin. Sindh specialises in this kind of phulkaries and is reputed to be its home.

The designs used indicate the influence of the Punjab as well as Kutch in the type of stitches used and the colours selected. The Phulkari work of upper Sindh seems to follow Punjabi Phulkari, while that of the Lower Sindh bears a resemblance to the Kutch work. Besides the button-hole stitch, the darning stitch of Kutch are also used in the Shishedar Phulkaries.

Kutch Phulkari

This is a name given to the embroidered silk or satin material used for skirts in Kutch. The popular figures chosen by the Kutch artist for embroidery are elephants, peacocks and parrots. Most of the embroidery is done in chain stitch, but occasionally herringbone stitch is also used for finishing the edge of the border.

Chamba Roomals

The Roomals of Chamba, a state in the Himalayan range are remarkable pieces of embroidery. Princesses as well as shepherdesses are equally adept in the art which they have adapted as a pleasant or profitable pastime for their leisure hours. The Roomal is a square piece of cotton material of the size of a teapoy cover. The material generally selected is very fine and of delicate lustre. The embroidery is worked in double satin stitch which produces the design on both sides of the material and so a Chambal Roomal does not have a right or wrong side.

The motifs for designs are figures, flowers, leaves, forming a sort of frame to set off the central representation of a scene from a mythological story or a legend. It is said of that embroidery that it "imitates the Pahari School of Painting". The unique characteristic of the embroidery is that it gives a vivid impression of the embroidered figure being in action or in motion, thereby enhancing the artistic value of the Roomals.

Kanthas of Bengal

Kanthas are not original fabrics, but are made with lengths of old and practically used up cloth. Several pieces of about the same length are placed one on top of another and the edges of all the pieces are sewn together so as to form a padded or quilted rectangular piece. Then the artist proceeds to depict beautiful patterns or scenes from stories, from the epics or well known legends, by means of embroidery done in simple running stitch. The work is very fine and neat and accurately executed entirely from memory without the help of any tracing or drawing any written notes. The Kanthas are therefore classed as works of art and one has only to look at them to agree.

The women of Bengal often devote their leisure hours in working Kanthas, creating beautiful and artistic fabrics out of worn out clothes.

Embroidered Fabrics of Kashmir

Embroidered fabrics of Kashmir are world famous. The Pashmina shawls, the silk sarees, the Namdas and the various other silk and woollen articles are praised as work of art. The Kashmir embroidery is known as Kasheeda, and the stitches used are the satin stitch, the stem stitch and the loop stitch. The darning stitch is also used. The herringbone stitch is used for the edges of the finished pieces.

The craftsmen, in Kashmir, are generally men and are invariably assisted by boys often of a tender age, who do the actual embroidery. It is interesting to observe the young boys at work. The master craftsman calls out from the design before him, the kind and the number of stitches to be put in. As the instructions are called out the boys work swiftly and deftly with needles, and the stitches are completed almost as soon as the master has finished calling them out. The scene resembles that of a small class in a school with the boys taking down the dictation of the teacher.

Nature's bounteous gifts appear to have been literally showered on Kashmir and it is considered by many to be the nearest approach to "a paradise on earth". Kasheeda artists, therefore, under the inspiration of the beauty of the natural surroundings, have succeeded in reproducing it in their embroidery with such amazing skill, that in the words of Smt. Kamala Dongerkerry, "competes with the wealth of Nature's charms". The Kashmir artist has an inexhaustible treasure of motifs in gorgeous colours, ready at hand from which he can draw his designs. In Kashmir embroidery, therefore, we find bunches of fruits, foliage and birds of brilliant hues and innumerable shades of colour which lend-themselves as charming compounds of varied designs. The Turanj (or the mango) is not ignored either. Indeed, it finds a place in almost all the Kasheedas of Kashmir.

The outstanding characteristics of Kashmir embroidery is its elegance and the harmonious group of the brilliant colours in the design which produces a restful and soothing effect. The workmanship is so neat and the stitches so fine that one wonders how bare human hands and that too of young boys could produce such work. It must however be remembered that training of generations (the craft is handed down from father to son in each of the families) has equipped the artisans with almost an intuitive aptitude for the work which has become second nature to them. On the other hand the art lives only as long as, it is in the family. This, alas, is what started to happen some time ago mainly due to the rage for replacing human hands by lifeless machinery. Paradoxical as it might appear science is fast stifling and killing art by restricting the scope of arts creation only to such articles which end themselves in mass production by mechanised processes.

The modern products of Kashmir are no longer as fine and delicate as in the past, and tend to lose their natural charm.

The embroidery is best done in silk but the identical patterns are also repeated in wool. Besides the Pashmina shawls and the silk sarees, the industry produces many articles for use in the home.

Namdas are the embroidered rugs. The rug is a felted thick fabric manufactured by the process of pressing wool and cotton together. They are then embroidered in thick wool in bright coloured designs similar to those on Pashmina. Kashmir silk embroidered fabrics besides being colourful and rich in design and comparatively inexpensive, are within the means of middle class people. Thus a wider patronage supports the industry and the art has flourished not by the patronage of the great and the rich alone.

Chikankari Embroidered Muslins

The white embroidery on white cotton especially on muslin is known as Chikan work. Chikankari is an industry nurtured and developed in the region watered by Ganga and her sister Yamuna (Jamuna). Lucknow in particular is the cradle and unrivalled centre of the art.

Chikan work lack in the attractiveness associated with colour yet has a fascination of its own, unequalled by few and surpassed by none. Whilst the Kasheeda of Kashmir may be rich in colour. Reflecting in silk the ravishing beauty with which Nature has gifted the valley, the virgin white Chikankari is perhaps a translation in simple cotton of the purity of the waters of the sister rivers born in the home of perpetual snows, the Himalayas. Much credit for the high position of the art of the Kashmir embroidery goes to its attractive colours. The fact that without that colourful aid, the Chikankari has attained the same eminence, is eloquent of its great artistic value.

Daintiness and delicacy (which are hallmarks of all Lucknow works of art) added to a finish and a richness of its own, are the outstanding characteristics of Chikankari. The work is sometimes so fine that to the naked eye it presents the appearance of having been woven-in, along with the fabrics.

There are two main styles of Chikan embroidery:

1) The flat—this group includes the bukhia and the katao styles.

2) The knotted or the embossed, of which the murri and the phanda are the well-known varieties. To these may be added a third style namely, the jali or netting which is akin to the drawn-thread-work, but is produced in an entirely different way. The different way. The drawing out of threads is regarded slovenly by the jali embroiderers, instead, the fabric is pierced with holes of the requisite size to suit the pattern and these are then tied to produce an appearance of net. Jalis are of different kinds variously named, Madras Jali, Calcutta Jali etc., and are very elaborate and intricate.

The varieties of designs are said to be thirty in number. Considering the fact that the colours are not used to vary the designs, and only the forms and motifs alone produce the various patterns, the number is creditable. The design represents familiar objects connected with daily life, often grains like rice and millet, in a variety of combinations.

The bukhia is the most remarkable of Chikan designs. It is supposed to be the true Chikan. Shrimati Kamla S. Dongerkerry considers it "comparable to the shadow work of the present day" and thus describes the technique of its production. The stitches in this design cover the back of the cloth in the style of the herringbone stitch, producing an effect on the surface of the fine white fabric and at the same time an outline of motifs flowers and leaves with minute stitches resembling the strokes of the back stitch.

The Katao produces an effect similar to bukhia. The same fabric is used to produce an opaque effect and for the outline a simple ordinary stitch is used.

The murri and the phanda are used mostly in the patterns representing grains.

Chikankari

Work is mostly used for saree borders, blouses or kurta collars and till recent times it was also used for the neck pieces, the cuffs, and even the hems of men's angrakhas (long coats). It has lately come into use as table linen, tes-cosy covers, and numerous other washable articles of domestic use. Probably due to the influence of the Western customers who invariably look for colour in Eastern products, the embroiderers have begun to use coloured threads to a little extent which, alas deteriorates the pristine elegance of the spotless white.

Costumes and Fashion

CHAPTER 9

Ancient Egyptian Dress

Clothing was not in any way a practical necessity in Ancient Egypt. Egypt (and most of the rest of North Africa) was not the mainly desert country it is today, subject to the temperature extremes that a dry climate engenders. Then it was a lush, food-producing country, subject to annual flooding, and a warm, humid climate. Clothing was therefore a luxury item of no great practical value. Slaves and the poor in surviving Ancient Egyptian art are therefore usually depicted in little more than loincloths. As people went up the social scale more clothing and jewelry was worn, but even then the drapery of the clothing is light and designed more to accentuate the shape of the body than conceal it. The most elaborate Egyptian clothing was worn by the Pharaohs and their queens as symbols of power.

It is thought by some that royal Egyptians practiced body modification by wrapping the skulls of infants and altering the head shape to be more egg like than rounded in adulthood, others ascribe this to a natural genetic fluke in the royal family. Aristocratic Egyptians also often shaved their heads (and other body hair) and wore wigs instead of natural hair to formal occasions. Kohl eye makeup was worn by both sexes, as were perfumes and body oils. During banquets, guests wore small mounds of beeswax impregnated with perfumed oil on top of their wigs; these mounds would melt into the wigs with the heat of the room, releasing scent, during the course of the party. Jewelry was the dominant costume focus, worn by both sexes; numerous examples of Ancient Egyptian jewelry survive in museums. Clothing has been less fortunate in survival, but linen textile scraps remain to indicate that the mostly white pleated materials that are shown in Ancient drawings were probably fine linens. These pleated linen garments are usually depicted as straight pieces of cloth, pleated to give a body-hugging stretch, that are wrapped in a variety of ways and tied or tucked in front.

Ancient Greek Dress

Ancient Greek dress was more voluminous than that of the Egyptians, and was most often made of fine woolens, although it is thought that the Greeks also had regular access to linen, hemp cloth and silk. The primary garment of Ancient Greek clothing was the Chiton, an all-over body garment made from a large rectangle of cloth wrapped once around the body from right side to left side. This garment was then pinned at the shoulders and tied at the waist or hips, and draped in hanging folds about the body. Young men generally wore short chitons, and older men and women longer ones. Older men also often are depicted wearing long draped mantles either alone or over a chiton. A smaller rectangle worn over one shoulder by travelers and young men was called a Chalmys. Women's Chitons were draped in a variety of ways, and were also worn with mantles. Greek fabric was far more elaborate than the Egyptians, and included complex border designs both woven in and embroidered. Greek jewelry, although less prominent than Egyptian jewelry, was exceedingly complex and finely made. Like Egyptian dress, Greek clothing was centered in an aesthetic that idealized the human body, rather than attempting to conceal it's natural shape. The Greeks made many clothing decisions based on this aesthetic that were less than practical choices: Pinning garments closed instead of stitching, rarely wearing sandals or shoes despite a rocky landscape, draping garments around the body for warmth during cold instead of making garments with sleeves or trousers as their near neighbours the Phrygians did. The Greeks definitely knew how to make sleeves, for their theatrical costumes had them, but for normal wear sleeves were judged less aesthetic than bare arms and so were not worn. Greek jewelry was also an object of much technical concentration, so much so that tern jewellery technique has only caught up to it since the Industrial Revolution.

Ancient Roman Dress

Sandals/Boot

At first glance appears to be identical to Greek dress in it's draperies and design. Closer inspection, however, reveals many important changes. First, the basic garments are sewn, not pinned, and close on both sides. Second, elaborate fabric decoration nearly disappears, and bold patterns on garments are nonexistent. Sandals, boots and shoes are common, virtually all men wear them, and many women. Jewellery becomes so simple in design and execution it looks crude, even without the comparison of the fine Greek work standing in contrast to it.

Contrary to the views engendered by sensational fiction such as Bulwer Lytton's "Last Days of Pompeii" or the wondrous silliness of Romans were, by and large, the kind of practical, upright, uptight folks who believed in civil service, interstate highways, and customs duties. Their clothing included the Tunica (which is, as you have already guessed, a simple t-tunic), the Stola (the female version of the same thing), the Toga (an extra long half-circle wool mantle worn by male citizens) and the Palla, a large, long (8 yard) drape or scarf worn by women outdoors. Sartorial decadence, such as it was, centered around women's hairstyles which changed fashion regularly and were often elaborately silly.

Dress in the French Revolution and the Periods

This time frame from 1789-1825 is actually several different sub-periods. The first, 1789-1799, the period of The French Revolution, is a sharp transition period. The second 1800-1815 is the time of the French Consulate and Empire, and is a stable Neo-classical period. 1815-1825 is the late Neo-classical period that shows a gradual shift towards the Romantic style.

Dress in the French Revolution

Roman woman's hair

Late 18th century women's dress collapses from it's padded and puffed look to a thin, often translucent silhouette. As the French Revolution progressed, different women's styles were adopted that appeared to have reference to the revolutionary politics, social structure and philosophy of the time. In the early 1790's, for example, the "English" or man-tailored style was favoured as it hinted towards the leanings of constitutional monarchy. There was a brief fashion for plain dresses in dark colors during the Terror of 1792, but when the Directory took over French fashion again went wild, trying out Rosseasque fashions in "Greek", "Roman", "Sauvage" and "Otaheti" (Tahitian) styles. The Psudo-"Greek" look proved most popular and was adopted as the standard style in Europe in the late 1790's.

While Men's Costume in the 1790's also becomes thinner in line, it separates it's style from women's dress by beginning to lose nearly all forms of surface decoration, lace and bright color, as "irrational" and feminine effluvia. This change is slow, but it completely alters men's dress by the mid 19th century into dull dark uniform dress.

Other major changes include the adoption of trousers from the dress of sailors and the urban proletariat of the French Revolution, the passing of the fashions for wigs and hair powder, and the (very temporary) demise of the corset.

The bonnet is invented as a hat that is meant to look like a Greek helmet, but it quickly is altered in style out of all resemblance to the original.

The Neoclassical Era (1800-1825)

Probably due to post-revolutionary backlash against female influence in politics, later reinforced by the German Philosopher Shopenhauer (who promoted the view that men were supposed to be rational and women emotional), the sexual dichotomy in dress becomes more pronounced in this era, a trend which continues through the 19th century. The direction of fashions towards Neoclassic dress for women, and increasingly drab utilitarian dress on men, continue in a steady manner in this very stylistically stable period. Women's dress locks into a pattern of light colored muslin gowns, high waisted with little puffed sleeves, and psudo-Greek hairstyles, which achieved an apex at the coronation of the Emperor Napoleon in 1804. As the period proceeds, the originally simple lines of these gowns are increasingly decorated with ruffles and puffs, the skirts get puffed out with petticoats, the waist lowers and tightens with corsets, until by 1825 it is hard to see how the style worn was ever imagined to look Greek. Men's dress also keeps on a fairly steady course towards increasing dullness. Fashion magazines continue to push men's dress towards foppish extremes, but men who actually count in the fashionable world tend to push for plainer styles. Beau Brummell the leader of male sartorial fashion in England in this period was noted for wearing only black with a white shirt for formal evening wear, a marked departure from the style of the previous century. Tubular and fitted trousers also move from a radical fashion statement to everyday wear for most men of the upper classes.

Terms used for clothing during French Revolutions

CHAPTER 10

♦	Aba	Open fronted coats probably derived from the name of coarse fabrics.
♦	Acuchillados	Spanish name for slashing.
♦	Agal	Head gear consist of a scarf wound round the head and held in place by its own fringes tucked into the roll.
♦	Alb	Long white linen tunic.
♦	Albarian hat	Hat popularized the Portraits of Henri IV. It had a high crown, raised front and trimmed with the feature.
♦	Amadis sleeve	Tight fitted sleeve continuing from the back of the hand which was found in 19th century.
♦	Amictus	The generic term applied to all draped garments in ancient Rome.
♦	Amigaut	Slit made at the neck of the garment for both male and female easier to put on. Also a decorative panel in front of the arm hole.
♦	Anaxyrides	Greek name for Persian long trousers.
♦	Apron	Plain piece of cloth which is tied by the women round the waist to preserve the gowns.
♦	Attiffet	Women head gear of 16th century formed an arc on either sides of the forehead and covered by a falling veil over the brow.
♦	Aumusse	A simple head dress in the form of flat hood falling on the shoulders worn by both the sexes.
♦	Bagnolette	Little hooded cape fastened under the chin and at foot with

gathers; sometime it was also gather at the neck in a little cape covering the shoulders.

- Baigneuse — Finely tucked large bonnet worn in the bath.
- Balandran — Medieval rain cape of France.
- Bamberges — Shinguards of Carolingian period.
- Banyan — Men Jacket in Indian linen cloth which is an indoor wear.
- Bar Bet — Veil fixed above the ears either to hair, chin and neck which is compulsory to nuns.
- Bas De Cotte — Term used for the lower part of the skirt.
- Basquine — Skirt similar to umbrella skirt.
- Batlamt — Head dress who sides projects well in front of the face, temple and eyes.
- Beluque — A Type of woman's mantle.
- Beret — A Round woolen cap, flat or full volumed.
- Bi Bis — A type of bonnet but much less voluminous than hat.
- Biretta — A head dress worn by the clergy.
- Birrus — Garment forming a hooded cloak made up of rough cloth, worn by Romans.
- Blanchet — Long cotton camisole with collar and sleeves.
- Bliaud — Long over gown worn by both sexes.
- Bloomers — Women trousers.
- Boater — A round, flat topped hat.
- Bodice — A part of womans garment from shoulder to waist.
- Boemio — Three quartered length cape worn by men in Spain.
- Bolero — Short Jacket.
- Bonnet — The stuff used for making all types of head wear.
- Boot — The term referred to a type of slippers.
- Boot Hose — Very long stockings worn with boots.
- Boule Vart — Short upper hose attacked to the belt.
- Bourdalou — Fine ribbon type of trimming used to round the crown of hat.

♦	Bourrelet	The cloth stuffing used as a component for various purposes in head dresses.
♦	Bowler hat	Men's hat with medium heighted crown, which was fashionable towards 1863 as a very small hat.
♦	Braces	A tube woven containing tiny springs made up with ribbon and cord used with the waist coats.
♦	Bractiates	Fastening pins used by the Mero Vingians.
♦	Branc	Women's smock, worn especially in 15th century.
♦	Brassard	It was the part of the sleeve from the wrist to elbow, joined to the mancheron of the upper sleeve by ribbons.
♦	Breeches	Term first used in Britain which formerly known as hose, upper-stock, slops.
♦	Culotte	A type of trousers or short pants worn by man which now known as divided skirts which is in fashion.
♦	Brigandine	Doublet of cloth or leather covered by leaves or scales of metals, covered in turn with leather or cloth which is held by the rivet of this triple sheath together.
♦	Broad cloth	Any unpatterned one-coloured cloth.
♦	Brocattelle	Originally a small patterned brocade, made up by mixture of silk, cotton, wool without silver/Gold which has a little value.
♦	Brodequin	Strap stocking worn inside the boots for weapon practice.
♦	Broigne	War garments made up of leather or strong linen reinforced with metal or horn.
♦	Buckrain	Man's padded great coat with fairly wide sleeve, in fashion in 1850.
♦	Bukingham	Man's hat; a sort of cap with two visors, one flat and the other raised, worn in imitation of Bukingham troops.
♦	Buff Jerkin	A sort of Jacket, with or without sleeves made up of cloth/leather or hide was the military costume.
♦	Bustle	Also called Dress improver, worn under the skirt supporting to back of skirt.
♦	Caban	Probably the first fitted coat with sleeves introduced to Europe from East Venice.

◆ Cache Folies — Small wigs worn in early 19th century to camouflage the cropped heads of women who had adopted the 'Titus' hairstyle after the revolution.

◆ Captan — A prototype of garment wraped with fitted back and front open.

◆ Calasiris — Egyptian tunic shaped robe in semi-transparent white linen with sewn at the sides with or without pleats and was held by knotted belt at the waist.

◆ Calceus — Roman shoe or half boot covering the foot and sometimes the leg upto calf level.

◆ Cale — A sort of beguin hood with two ribbons knotted under the chin.

◆ Calecheor Cabrio Let — An adoption of fashionable over coats with draw strings into wide capes protecting the head.

◆ Caliga — An enclosed shoe with a thick, nailed solo covering foot and lower leg, worn by Roman soldiers.

◆ Calyptra — Head dress of the Byzantire emperor in the form of an arched Polygon.

◆ Cameleurion — Hemispherical crown worn by Caesars.

◆ Camlet — Camel hair fabric made originally in Asia.

◆ Cammocas — A very beautiful silk cloth, often striped with gold and silver with a satin base.

◆ Campagus — Shoe which had a very high quarter fitted on the corners above the ankles, with laces which tied over the instep.

◆ Canezou — Small quimp with/without sleeves, its main feature was that it was tucked into the belt.

◆ Canons — The Canons are the sort of half stockings at first long and narrow, then wider and decorated with flounces and lace worn between nether hose and the boot.

◆ Cap — Man's head dress, flat and round, and always with a peak.

◆ Capa — Wide circular hooded cloak worn by men in Spain in 16th to 17th centuries.

◆ Capote — A woman head-wear fitted closely round the chignon, with a wide flaring brem framing the face.

◆ Cappa flocata — Round cap in hairy material, still worn by Greek shepherds.

◆	Cappuccio	Italian name for the hood.
◆	Caracalla	A narrow, tight-fitted garment, sometimes hood, with long sleeves, it was split in front and behind to the groin.
◆	Caroco	Is the french provincial costume, the essential gown, cut off at hip level and forming a sort of short, peasant-style jacket.
◆	Carbatina	The commonest type of ancient footwear, a piece of oxhide forming a sole turned up round the edges and over the toes and held over the instep by laces passed through holes pierced in the leather.
◆	Carcaille	A flaring collar, rising to the ears.
◆	Carmagnole	Jacket worn by French Revolutionaries in 1792-1793.
◆	Carrick	Originally a coachman's heavy coat; a box-coat.
◆	Cassock	A sort of unbelted over coat, three quarter length, with long or short slit sleeves, open-sided and almost invariably covered with braid and woven ornament.
◆	Cendal	Silk material resembling taffeta, made in various qualities, luxurious fabric, cheap lining material.
◆	Chaconne	Type of cravat made of a ribbon dangling from the shirt collar to the chest.
◆	Chaddar or Uttariya	Indo-Iranian shawl or mantle.
◆	Chainse or Cainsil	A long tunic of fine linen cloth with long sleeves tight-fitted at the wrists; usually finely pleated.
◆	Chamarre	A long, wide coat, open in front, with full-topped sleeves, furlined and heavily decorated with braid, worn by Spanish shepherds.
◆	Chapeau-Bras	To avoid disarranging their wigs, elegants developed the habit of carrying their hats in their hands and then under the left-arm.
◆	Chaperon	Hood with short cape. Known as a collet.
◆	Charlotte	Large woman's hat, named after queen Charlotte of England; a wide tightly-gathered crown, the brim covered with a generous flounce.
◆	Chasuble	Originally an outer garment, circular in shape with an opening for the head, generally without a hood.
◆	Chausse	Alternative name for the epitoga.
◆	Chausses En Bourses	Early 17th century breeches made in bands and padded so they

swelled out at bottom, ending in a flattened balloon shape.

◆ Chemise	A light under garment for both sexes.
◆ Chemise Gown	A muslin gown with sleeve fitting tightly at wrist, fitted at the waist but loose at throat, opened front fastened with pin and ribbon sash at waist.
◆ Cherusque	Name given to the stretched lace collarettes of court costume.
◆ Child's Pudding	Small round hat for children made of cloth or straw, forming a shock-absorber to protect them if they fell.
◆ Chintz	Linen, originally Persian, printed and wax-glazed often wrongly called glazed percale.
◆ Chite	Painted linen originally from India in 17th and 18th century.
◆ Chiton	Ancient Greek garment made up of linen, then a tunic of that cloth. Essentially an under garment, leaving the right shoulder bare, or held over both shoulders by fibula.
◆ Chlaine	Woolen cloak of Homeric period, worn by shepherds and warriors.
◆ Chlamys	Short, light Greek garment, trapeze shaped. Originally from Thessaly.
◆ Chopines	Spanish name for the raised pattens worn by women to increase their height.
◆ Cingulum	Band or belt worn by women beneath the breasts, to grid in the tunic and also belt used by men for active exercise at hips.
◆ Circassienne	A variant of the gown; it had three back panels, differing from polonaise by its very short sleeves which exposed the long or half-length sleeves of the under-bodice.
◆ Clavi	Purple bands which ran vertically from each shoulders to the foot decorating the tunic of Roman dignitaries.
◆ Chebwig	About 1785 a man's wig with one pigtail tied with a narrow ribbon and with a bulge at the end; women took up this hair style and wore either single or double cadogans. The style returned to fashion, particularly for young girls who had not yet put up their hair, in the late 19th and early 20th centuries.
◆ Coat of Arms	Sort of long tunic strengthened with metal rings, worn from the 11th century onwards.
◆ Codpiece	A piece of cloth designed to cover the opening of the hose,

attached by two buckles to the front of hose. Also served as pocket.

- Colf — Piece of linen or cloth following the shape of the head and worn under the helmet or hood.

- Coiffure En Bouffons — Women's hair-style; tufts of crimped hair over the temples, while the forehead was covered by fringe known as garcette.

- Coiffure En Bourse — "It was the fashion taken from horses"; men's hair was held in a little black ribbon bag tied with a rosette, also called as Bag wig.

- Coiffure En Cadenettes — Hair styles invented by the Sire de Cadenet which entailed letting a lock of hair (a 'moustache') fall on either side of the face; these were wound with ribbons and tied with a bow. Worn by both sexes.

- Coiffure En Raquette — Women's hair style with hair swept up all round the face, puffed out over the temples and supported by a hoop.

- Collet Monte or Rotonde — After the ruff men wore a linen collar with a cord or tin base. Women also wore a standing, fan shaped, lace trimmed collar.

- Colobium — Sort of blouse or sleeveless coat worn in Ancient Gaul.

- Combinations — Several articles of underwear joined into one; Bodice-Pantaloon Petticoat.

- Comperes — Small false front in two pieces fixed to the edge of the bodice and simulating a waist coat.

- Conch — Sort of large shell-shaped hat in gauze, mounted on a tin framework with a similar veil much bigger made of pale gauze.

- Cope — Originally a hooded cloak designed for protection against rain.

- The University Gown — Rather different from the civilian cloak, was closed, and had two slits on the front or sides for the arms to pass through.

- Cordoban Leather — Goat skin, simply-tanned but not with gall like the leather they call Morocco. The art of preparing this leather came from Cordoba and the craftsmen allowed to use it for making shoes in the middle ages.

- Cornet — The more or less point of the hoods still worn by French peasants and nuns. The name was also used for the ornaments, hoops and bands round the crown of the hat.

- Cornet hat — Women's hat with gathered crown and narrow brim, fashionable in the Directoire period.

◆	Corps pique	Women wore a sort of quilted camisole fitted with a bust or busk of varnished wood to stiffen it; inspiration of Spanish fashion.
◆	Corset	Long or short surcoat with or without sleeve worn by men and women wore gowns laced in front and furlined for winter.
◆	Cotehardie	Mens surcoat open in front, split and buttoned at the sides, with wide sleeves.
◆	Coteron	Little coat, worn by the people; a sort of fatigue coat.
◆	Cothurnes	High boots worn by huntsmen.
◆	Coureur	Very tight fitting caraco with very short basques, worn by women during the Revolutionary period.
◆	Cramignole	Man's cap with turned up brim made up of velvet and trimmed with pompoms, feather etc.
◆	Cravat	Ornamental neck wear which was inspired in 1668 by a Croatian regiment.
◆	Cremona Cravat	Cravat which was decorated with gathers of a plain ribbon along each edge.
◆	Crepida	A Greek shoe similar to the Roman carbatina, formed by a thick sole with a narrow piece of leather covering the sides of the boot, pierced along the top with several holes through which a thong passed attaching it to the instep. Sometimes the edges had leather buckles through which the strips passed.
◆	Criardes	Under skirts of gummed linen prefiguring paniers, worn in early 17th century.
◆	Crinoline	Cloth of horse hair and woven for officer's collars, and then used for civilain collars in the Romantic period.
◆	Crispin	Coat without collar or armholes designed in 1826 to protect actresses waiting in the wings from draughts; adopted by men, women and children.
◆	Crotalia	Fanciful name given by Roman ladies to earrings made of several pear-shaped beads, large enough to make sounds like castanets.
◆	Cucullus	Name given in Rome to the hoods of working clothes.
◆	Cuerpo Baxo	Spanish name for the quilted, boned, sleeveless bodice worn in the 16th century.
◆	Culot	Very short tight breeches worn during the reign of Henri III.

- Chaussures — Shoes with heels so called because they resembled abridge raised by a Jack.

- Dabiki — In 15th century Dabiki, a suburb of Damietta, produced robes woven with gold and linen turbans embroidered with gold, in stuff so light that fifty yards of dabiki could go into one turban.

- Daggings — 15th century German fashion; adopted mainly at the court of Burgundy; the hems of garment and sleeves, the ends of bands etc. were cut in various patterns—toothed, with long cut-out leaves and even, inside the leaves, bands of pertuise work-cut open-work in small patterns.

- Dalmatic — Long, wide sleeved blouse falling to the feet in white Dalmation wool decorated with vertical purple bands, adopted as part of Christian liturgical dress.

- Damask — Originally a silk fabric made in Damascus, with self-coloured patterns of flowers, branches, and animals in satin finish contrasting with the slightly textured taffeta background. Multi-coloured damasks are lampas.

- Damaskin — A sort of brocatelle or multi-coloured damask with flower motifs in gold and silver.

- Devantiere — 17th century; woman's riding costume split at the back.

- Device — A figured object or emblem adopted as a distinguishing sign in middle ages.

- Dhoti — Indo-Iranian loin-cloth. Wrap on the waist by men.

- Diphtera — Cretan cloak formed of an animal skin or thick woolen cloth cover-ing the shoulders.

- Dogaline — A straight loose gown worn by men and women, it featured a very wide sleeve whose lower edge was fastened up to the shoulder.

- Dormeuse — Cap with a ruched border fitting tightly to the head, held by a ribbon tied on the top of the head worn at night.

- Doublet/Pourpoint — Originally a quilted garment padded with cotton or waste, held in place by stitching—worn by men in early 14th century.

- Drawers — Under garment worn by ladies and mens drawer were made in linen in 16th century.

- Duck Bill Shoes — Exaggeratedly wide shoes, which succeeded the Poulaine in the late 15th-16th centuries.

◆ Engageantes	Lace cuffs with two or three tiered ruffles, finishing women's gown sleeves still worn in 18th century.
◆ Ephod	A sort of corselet supported by shoulder straps and worn by the Jewish high priest; then used in Christian Priestly Costume during the first years of Christianity.
◆ Epitoga	Originally a cloak, worn over the toga, a wide, ungathered unbelted robe, sometimes with bell sleeves.
◆ Escaffignons	Very little flat shoes, generally slashed on top. The term already existed in the 12th century for a light shoe in rich material.
◆ Escoffion	Wrongly given by some authors as the name for tall hairstyles covered by a net snood, worn in the early 15th century.
◆ Estrain	Straw used for hat-making in the middle ages.
◆ Exomide	Very short sleeveless Greek tunic completely open down the right side.
◆ Faces	Flat locks of hairs framing the face of Dandies in the Directoire period.
◆ Facings	Edging of fine fur or rich cloth, used to face fine garments for lining.
◆ Falling Ruff	Last form of the ruff in France during the reign of Henri IV; unstarched and falling in tiers on the shoulders.
◆ False Gown	Fashion of England borrowed from French little girl's styles and converted it into a womens dress. It consisted of a tight bodice with skirt gathered all round. A broad ribbon tied at the back formed a belt. It is called a false gown because it did not have an overgown open over a petticoat but was in one piece.
◆ False Sleeves	In the 14th century, the habit of letting the unbuttoned lower part of sleeves hang down gave rise to this fashion; long panels fell from the elbow, sometimes to ankle-length. Originally an integral part of the sleeve, they were later sewn to the sleeve, and were sometimes in contrasting fabrics.
◆ Farthingale	Spanish fashion of the late 15th century introduced in France in 16th century. A coorse linen underskirt was stretched over thick iron wire which supported the skirts.
◆ Feminlia	Short drawers attached at the waist and reaching knees worn by

the Roman troops serving in cold northern climates.

◆ Ferreruolo — Long cape with velvet collar and no hood worn by Spanish men in 16th century.

◆ Ferroniere — Small jewel attached to a fine chain holding it on the forehead.

◆ Fibula — Pin or brooch used in ancient times to attach or fasten male and female garments.

◆ Fichu — Small black lace scarf which women knotted around their necks so that the points fell on the chest. This term came from the long leather loop which hung from horses croups in the middle ages to aid mounting.

◆ Fichu Menteur — Fichu worn by women in the neck of coats and open dresses; it was draped so that it exaggerated the figure and increased the size of the bust.

◆ Fiettro — Men's three quarter length cape with high collar and hood, worn in 16th century in Spain.

◆ Flammeum — Marriage veil worn by Roman brides on their wedding day. It was dark flame colour and covered the wearer from head to foot throughout the ceremony. The bridegroom removed it only on reaching their newhome.

◆ Flounce — A band of cloth or lace fluting round a garment to which it is attached only by its upper edge.

◆ Fontanges Head-Dress — About 1678, women's hairstyle, with the hair swept up and held by a ribbon which was modified with complicated cap and various accessories.

◆ Frac — An informal men's garment wider than the coat without outer pockets and with a turned down collar in 1767 till 19th century.

◆ Frock Coat — English garment with formal Embroidered coats; knights models often had several collars.

◆ Full Bottomed Wig — Light wig, with three locks of hair.

◆ Fustian — Cloth of cotton or blended with linen which is used for under garments and lining.

◆ Galabijeh — Modern gown worn by Egyptian fellahin.

◆ Galerus — In Rome, a rounded cap of animal skin worn by peasants and hunts-men. A cape of the same shape but made of the skin of sacrificed animals with an olive wood point was reserved for pontiffs.

◆ Gallants — Small ribbon bows worn in the hair and scattered about the clothes.

◆ Gallicae — Low Gaulish shoe with one or more thick soles, the upper exposing the instep, sometimes laced on top.

◆ Gambeson — Quilted, padded garment worn under armour.

◆ Gamurra — Italian women's garment, often mentioned but never clearly described.

◆ Garde-Corps — Garment for both sexes, which in the early 14th century replaced the surcoat or was worn over it, normally loose and flowing, often sleeveless or with short wide sleeves, and disappeared at the end of 14th century.

◆ Garnache — Surcoat or robe worn for extra warmth; similar in shape to the HOUSSE.

◆ Garnement — Each of the individual pieces composing a robe.

◆ Garters — Ribbon tied round the leg to hold up the stocking.

Band, usually fastened with a buckle holding the edge of knee-breeches to the leg.

◆ Gipon — Was called as jupe, jupel, jupon in the middle ages. A sort of doublet made of padded and quilted material. It was an under garment and the breeches were attached to it.

◆ Girdle — A vividly coloured sash passing over the shoulders, crossed at the back and tied round the waist.

◆ Go Nelle — Long tunic, worn by both sexes in the Merovingian and Roman periods, it was adopted as Monastic Costume. It also became the long coat of knights. The male style reached only half way down the legs.

◆ Gorgerette — Any costume accessory covering the neck and throat, decorated in silk, wool, linen and fur.

◆ Gorgias — Gauze used in Late 15th century to mask the pronounced decollete of women's dresses; by extension, the plunging neckline itself and any other provocative elegance.

◆ Gown A La Francaise — The sack gown gave way to a dress consisting of a close-fitted bodice, opening in front on a traingular stomacher, which was generally richly decorated; at the back two large double pleats fell freely from the middle of the collar spreading to the ground.

♦ Gown A La Levatine

A gown so comfortable and so simple to put on and take off that it has earned the name, fastened on the chest with a pin; only the foot of the back was pleated; skirt opening from front; worn over an under garment whose amadis sleeves passed through the levantine's half-sleeves.

♦ Gown A Langlaise

A Gown in 1778-85 was stitched without boned bodice, characterised by a long boned point reaching down the middle of the back to below the waist. The front closed over a waist coat; the sides of the skirt opened on a petticoat usually of the same material.

♦ Gown Polonaise

One of the soft dresses of the last third of the 18th century. Characteristic features: fastened at the top of boned bodice, then cut away to show a tight fitting waist coat, sabot sleeves, over the underskirt it formed three draped panels held up by draw strings.

♦ Gown Sultane

Dress opening in front over an under skirt of a different colour.

♦ Gown Turque

Gown which by its elegances, caused crowds together at the Palais Royal when it first appeared. It had a tight bodice, with turned down collar, flaring sleeves, pleated corset and a draped belt knotted over one hip.

♦ Gown in Surgente

On of the fashions inspired by the American War of Independence; however, it was only a gown with Pagoda sleeves which was widely worn by Anglo-American women, in 17th century.

♦ Granatza

Long sleeved gown, originally Assyrian; the exact cut is unknown. The Persians transmitted it to the Byzantines.

♦ Great coat/overcoat

English surcoat/overcoat with a flat collar topped with a smaller collar that could be raised to protect the face.

♦ Greaves

A costume accessory covering the leg from ankle to knee.

♦ Guard Infanta

Large farthingale still worn in Spain in the 17th century.

♦ Gueridons

Paniers made of very large hoops fastened together with tape.

♦ Guimp

Originally a piece of light material with which women surrounded their face, letting it fall over their neck and chest. This term first would have referred to light silk cloth and become attached to the articles made of the stuff.

♦ Guleron	Part of the chaperon covering the shoulders.
♦ Habit	The two piece suit of clothes (doublet and breeches) or three piece with the mantle or four piece, with stocking, all in the same coloured or cloth.
♦ Haik Royal	Light pleated, carefully draped garment worn in Egypt by pharaoh's and queens, which covered the body though revealing by its transparency.
♦ Haincelin	Short houppelande which took its name from Charles VI first, it is different from the normal houppelande in that both its sleeves were embroidered where as it is only embroidered on one sleeve.
♦ Half-Beaver	In 17th and 18th centuries beaver hats were the most prized and the dearest; hats were made of a mixture.
♦ Hat pin	When the hat was no longer tied with ribbons under the chin, hat pins oppeared. They were long, so as to go through the crowns of all shapes of hats, and were more or less richly decorated at one end. The hat pin disappeared when short hair became fashionable.
♦ Helm/Helmet/Casque	Military head-gear made of metal or leather.
♦ Hennin	Insulting term used for tall horned head dresses, considered wrongly to have been the name of the hair styles and the tall conical hat.
♦ Herigaute	Type of housse or grade corps worn in the late 13th and early 14th centuries. It was open at the sides similar in shape to the dalmatic.
♦ Heuze/Houseaux	Tall leather thick soled boots sometimes leaving the end of the foot uncovered. Some covered-half the leg, others rose to mid thigh.
♦ Himation	Greek mantle, made from a large rectangle cloth which could be draped in various ways, worn by both sexes.
♦ Hoqueton	Tight-fitting padded tunic; it is a part of parade uniforms for some companies, and was often decorated with precious stones.
♦ Horned-Head Dress	Womens tall head dress of 14th and first third of the 15th centuries.
♦ Hose	Liturgical hose covering the foot and part of the leg, knitted or

	cut from cloth. They were divided into two such that the upper hose e.g., new underpant (shorts) and lower hose e.g., stocking.
◆ Houppelande	Full over dress, with wide flaring sleeves and a funnel shaped collar worn by men, women and children.
◆ Housse	Outer garment with wide short sleeves forming a cape, button in front with two little tabs below the neck.
◆ Huik	Heavy flemish mantle covering the head and body, later combined with flat felt hat which crowned with a little tuft on a stalk rising from a skull cap on the head.
◆ Huque	Outer garment, a short flowing robe, open at the sides, worn by military and civilian.
◆ Hurluberlu	Woman hair style in which short curls covered the entire head.
◆ Huve	Womens head dress. Sort of tapered cornet projecting, held to each side of the head by long pins. The folds fell over the neck.
◆ Indiennes	Name given to all Eastern painted and printed stuffs, whatever their country of origin.
◆ Indigo	In ancient times the most precious dye, popular and admired inspite of its high price. Its use spread after the discovery of the sea-route to the Indies by Vascodagama (1498) extracted from indigo and isotis (pastel) plants.
◆ Indumentum	In Rome, general term for any garment or accessory that covers the part of the body.
◆ Ipsi Boe	There was a colour 'Ipsi boe', a yellowish beige which enjoyed a great vogue.
◆ Ispahanis	Name given to precious cloths made in Almeria (Spain) by the Moravids.
◆ Jabot	Originally the neck opening of the chemise, and its lace trimmings, showing through the opening at the doublet.
	Mens cloth were trimmed in pleated Jabot and in womens cloth as lace or embroidery trimmings.
◆ Jack	Sort of padded military doublet made up of 30 superimposed layers of cloth, fitted closely to the torso, could be rich cloth when it is not worn by soldiers.
◆ Jacket	Men's garment, closely fitted, worn mainly by the poor. Considered as peasants garment.

♦ Jaquette — Women's jacket inspired by hunting jackets etc.

♦ Jerkin — King of outer doublet worn in England either sleeveless/loose sleeves in a rich cloth.

♦ Jockey — Flounce forming an Epaulette placed at the top of the sleeve.

♦ Journade — Sort of flowing cassock with wide slit sleeves, should have been a parade or display garment.

♦ Jubon — Long sleeved camisole buttoned all the way down often in panels.

♦ Jupe — Part of women's costume from waist to feet.

♦ Kakofnitch — Russian women's head dress in the form of a tiara or diadem.

♦ Kandys — Tight sleeved caftan.

♦ Kaunakes — Long hair fur belt worn in summer in pre-Agadean period.

♦ Kepresh — War head dress of the pharaoh, a tall tiara covered with projecting circles perhaps metal rings.

♦ Klaft — Pharaonic head dress in stripped cloth on which a sparrow hawk was woven.

♦ Kontush — Generally cut caftan-shaped mantle worn in Poland.

♦ Kyne — Greek soldiers helmet made out of leather.

♦ Lacerna — Flowing hooded cloak, open fronted with a buckle or brooch at the throat, wide enough to be worn over the toga.

♦ Landdrines — Boots with widely flared tops, reaching half way up the leg; soft enough to be turned up for riding.

♦ Languti — Indian Loin cloth.

♦ Leading strings/Tatas — Long narrow stripes of cloth attached to the shoulders of small children's dress.

♦ Leg-of-Mutton Sleeves — Sleeves worn with a huge puff at the top of the sleeve.

♦ Lignium — Linen loin cloth.

♦ Lodier — Thick padded and quilted wrap used to make a sort of roll, over the hips to increase their bulk. This mode was short-lived.

♦ Loin Cloth — Band of material wound round the hips like a short shirt and worn in the past and now by primitive people.

♦ Loros — Scarf worn by Byzantine emperors.

- ◆ Lower stocks — Silk or woolen cloth stockings showing beneath upper stock.

- ◆ Madder — Plant yielding a bright red dye.

- ◆ Mafors — Long narrow veil, generally covering the head and falling over the shoulders worn by women. (6th-11th centuries)

- ◆ Maheutres — Cylindrical pads used to trim the shoulders of tight gippon sleeve, to broaden the shoulders.

- ◆ Mancheron — This term was applied to any half sleeve whether it covered the upper or lower arm.

- ◆ Maniakes — Collar worn by Byzantine emperors.

- ◆ Manteau — Overdress, that was worn over the bodice and petticoat.

- ◆ Manteline — Short parade garment worn over the armour; usually richly decorated, sometimes hooded.

- ◆ Mantilla — A large shawl worn by women and widows, young girls, who had to cover their head so as to show only one eye. It covers only the head and shoulders, as it does now.

- ◆ Mantle — It was the most simple and widespread outer garment; a large rectangle of thick stuff gathered at the neck, without sleeves, often with hood whose shape round or pointed.

- ◆ Mappa — Large piece of cloth used to give signal at games or as a table napkin.

- ◆ Marlotte — Sort of half length mantle, completely open in front, the back falling in symmetrical folds, had very short puffed sleeve and standing ruffled collar worn by womens.

- ◆ Marramas — Cloth of gold, oriental in origin, made in Lucca, it was mainly for ecclesiastical ornament.

- ◆ Martingale Breeches — Breeches with a movable panel between the legs, held to the belt by buttons and points.

- ◆ Mask — Theatrical accessory of ancient times. Worn by women to protect the wearers complexion and preserve her incognito. It has various names according to the shape of the period.

- ◆ Mathilde — Broad, vertical band of embroidary decorating women's dress-fronts.

- ◆ Medici Collar — Name given to the women's standing collars, in 16th century.

- ◆ Menat — Egyptian necklace, particular emblem of the goddess Hathor.

◆	Military Tunic	Appears in military uniform of 17th century.
◆	Mitra	A scarf with tie-tapes at the ends, so that it could be worn in various ways according to the wearer's needs. It covered the head and framed chin and neck.
◆	Mitre	Derived from term Mitra; it was the first bishops wore a gold circlet, more or less ornate, which was later lined with the crown.
◆	Mobcap	Linen night cap worn by women; this cap had a pleated border, worn under large bonnet hats.
◆	Moufles or mitons	Fingerless gloves worn in Merovingian period, used for hunting or rough work.
◆	Muff	A band of fur or fur-lined fabric, protecting the hands from the cold.
◆	Muleus	Red or violet boot worn by Roman patricians who had served as Magistrates.
◆	Muslin	The first fabrics from Mosul were silk with gold.
◆	Nages	Black frieze skirts worn in full mourning.
◆	Norfolk Jacket	Jacket in English cloth, adopted by men for sport and travel and by boys for hiking dress. Main features are — half belt catching in full back.
◆	Olicula	Hooded cap worn by Roman women.
◆	Opera hat	Collapsible top hat flattened by an internal spring so that it could be carried under the arm.
◆	Paenula	In Rome a kind of round hooded blouse with an opening for the head, sometimes the front was split to the groin to facilitate walking. It was made in heavy materials or leather and was worn for travel in bad weather.
◆	Pagoda sleeves	Sleeves which had cuff reaching to the elbow narrow in, instead of flaring out like the wide cuffs.
◆	Paison	Greek name for the trousers worn by the Persian.
◆	Palatine	Little fur stole which takes its name from the princess Palatine worn in winter.
◆	Palla	This garment was draped like the peplos and generally open down one side but sometimes the sides were sewn up and used like any other garment.

◆ Pallium   A long square/rectangle piece of wool, draped and fastened at the neck or on the shoulders by a brooch.

◆ Panama   Hats which was finely worked poplar wood. They were soft straw hats with rounded crowns.

◆ Paniers   Under skirts stretched over the metal hoops.

◆ Pantalettes   From the end of the first empire to about 1865 little girls' pantaloons showed below the dress hem.

◆ Pantaloons   Women's under garment, linen or silk pants more sophisticated and acquired flounces of lace or embroidary at the foot.

◆ Paragaudion   Persian tunic which was decorated with band of embroidary with gold.

◆ Parti-coloured Dress   Garment divided vertically in half in two colours of cloth, was in vogue by 12th century till 14th century.

◆ Passacaille   Fashionable dance (passacaglia) whose name was given to the cord attaching the muff to the waist under Louis XIV.

◆ Passement   Original name given to all forms of lace in the 16th-17th centuries either in thread, silk or metal.

◆ Patagium   Long band of purple or gold decorating the fronts of women's tunics. Similar to the clavus worn by men.

◆ Patna   Printed cloth imported from Patna on the Ganges probably one of the first fabrics imported in 1640. Traders were Portuguese from Surah, north of Bombay.

◆ Pattens   Shoes, thick soled or raised on high heels, worn mainly in Spain; worn over the slipper and generally made of worked or decorated leather or velvet; also a shoe fitted with an iron blade, for skating.

◆ Peascod Belly   False hump of stuffing and cotton lengthened into a horn-shape which filled out men's doublets.

◆ Peel   Man's light jacket, in vogue in 1850.

◆ Pelerine   Name given to a short cape covering the shoulders, similar to those worn by Watteau's 'pilgrims'.

◆ Pelicon   Fur-lined garment worn between chemise and cote.

◆ Pelisse   Women's mantle related to the cape and the tippet, wide and padded, fur edged, with two arm slits, sometimes with a hood, worn for evening outings.

- Peplos — Large rectangle of cloth, the top folded down, round the torso and pinned on each shoulder, the right side was open and the edges of the material fell loose drapery. Worn by women.

- Perizoma — Short, close fitting trunks worn by the Etruscans, Iberians and Sardinians.

- Pero — Boot made of hairy undressed hide, worn by agricultural workers under the Romans.

- Perse — Painted cloth from the Coromandel Coast, thought to be Persian.

- Petasus — Flat-crowned, broad-brimmed hat taken from Greece by the Romans, it was held on by the strings tied under the chin or behind the head, it has seen with two wings in most representations of mercury.

- Petit Bord — Small, elaborately fashioned hat inspired by togues of the Renaissance period, but differed from them by variety of its shapes and trimmings.

- Petite Oie — Set of ribbons which was used to trim men's suits and which became very large when petticoat breeches were worn.

- Petits Bonshommes — Sort of fine linen bracelet made of several frills, used to edge of the sleeves of gowns.

- Pharos — One of the forms of the peplos worn by Greek women; belted at the waist.

- Pianelle — Italian shoe often defined as the carpet slipper, it is nonetheless adapted for outdoor wear, protected by pattens.

- Piccadils — Notches made in the sleeve openings and necks of garment.

- Pierrot — A small garment worn like a Caraco, but much more fancyful in cut and trimmings.

- Pigache — Shoe with long, upturned, pointed toe.

- Pileus — Felt cap with the point folded over, also in tubular cap worn by men in Rome.

- Plaid — Scottish national costume, made in heavy woolen material checked in the colours of the clan, was draped over the shoulders and worn round the waist.

- Pleureuses — From 1900 on, ostrich feathers with each strand lengthened with another strand, first gummed but later tied.

♦	Pockets	In middle ages clothes did not have pockets; objects were held in the split of the neck opening, in the corner of the hood and later in the cod piece which opened like a box.
♦	Points	Metal-tagged laces that replaced the sewn estaches, to attach the upper hose to the gippon or the doublet.
♦	Polos	Greek womens hat already worn in Daedalic Crete.
♦	Poncho	Large rectangle of unsewn cloth, with an opening in the centre of the head; a prototype of the simplest form of primitive garment, it was worn in the earliest periods and is still worn by many South American people.
♦	Porcupine	Style with the hair cut short and standing up like bristles in 1798.
♦	Postillon	Gathered or ruffled basque at the foot of the bodice back; very fashionable in 1860-61 still mentioned in 1888.
♦	Poufs An Sentiment	Women's voluminous hair styles on which the most varied trimmings might find a place.
♦	Poulaines	Shoes said to be in the Polish style which appeared at the end of 14th century.
♦	Powdering	The fashion of powdering wigs began under Louis XIV
♦	Pretintailles	Decoration for women's gown coloured materials cut out and appliqued to the gown.
♦	Princess Dress	One piece in front, all the fullness taken to the back over the cage which had lengthened backwards.
♦	Pshent	Cap in the form of a truncated cone worn by the pharoahs.
♦	Pudding-Basin Cut	15th century hair-style; the hair was shaved on the neck and temples, leaving a skull cap of hair on the top of the head.
♦	Purple	Dye extracted from the Murexbrandis. It was yellow when collected; exposure to sunlight turned it red, then deep violet.
♦	Pyjama	The name comes from Hindustani *epai-jama* which were known as Mughal breeches.
♦	Rabat	Collar of linen and lace worn over the doublet, it was an lingerie ornament worn on women's bodice.
♦	Rebato	Brass wire support worn in Spain by men and women to support the ruff, which was thus held at an unusual angle.

◆ Rebras   The equivalent of revers, whether the upturned brim of a hat or the revers of a coat, the cuff of a glove, or a lingerie ornament.

◆ Reticule   The transparent gowns of the Directoire period made no provisions for pockets.

◆ Revers   The turned back edge of a coat, waistcoat or bodice.

◆ Rheno   Very short coat in reindeer skin, typically Germanic, worn is Gaul during Merovingian period.

◆ Ricinium: Square Viel worn by Roman women on their heads for offering sacrifices and other occasions. The Iricinium was a smaller veil folded in half, worn on the head, particularly as a sign of mourning.

◆ Robe   Originally, all the funiture and effects belonging to a person; then his collection of clothes.

◆ Robe Anglaise   About 1880 to 1900, a child's dress.

◆ Robe de Chambre   It is simply a gown differing from the court gown and was admitted to the chambres of the royal apartments outside receptions and ceremonies.

◆ Robe Deguisee   Term used for garment in new and daring fashion reserved for the most elegant wear.

◆ Robe Gironnee   Loose dress with pleats fixed at the waist which fell like organ pipes.

◆ Robe Longue   Long costumes worn by academics and religious orders.

◆ Rochet   Small collarless coat worn in the Loui's XIII period. The sleeves reached no further than the elbow and split along their full length so that it could be turned insider out, ended up on the backs of buffoons in the Italian comedy.

◆ Rond   A sausage-shaped pad over which women built their hair.

◆ Ropa   Spanish women's outer garment, opening all the way down the front, with a straight collar and sleeves bouffant at the top.

◆ Ropilla   Doublet which is very close-fitting, half-length basques and hanging sleeves.

◆ Roquelaure   Large, full over coat with cape, called after the Duke of Roquelaure.

◆ Rowel   Round of yellow cloth or felt which was compulsory wear for Jews.

- ◆ Ruff — Costume accessory for both sexes. A pleated, starched collarette worn throughout Western Europe by late 16th and 17th centuries.

- ◆ Sable — The finest, rarest and most celebrated type of marten fur.

- ◆ Sable — A sort of cloth woven from very fine beads used in 18th century for shoes and small objects like purses, ornaments etc.

- ◆ Sabot Pantaloons — Pantaloons wide at the bottom; the close-fitting leg was turned up outside.

- ◆ Sabot sleeves — Sleeve of the gown fitting tightly over the elbow.

- ◆ Saccoz — Byzantine imperial robe.

- ◆ Sack Gown — A loose dress flaring out at the bottom, the back attached to the neck band with gathered or pleated.

- ◆ Sacristan — Light brass wire farthingale with five or six hoops.

- ◆ Sagum — Originally a cloak worn by ancient Celts. It was made from hairy cloth recalling goat skin, square or rectangular draped over the left shoulder and pinned on the right.

- ◆ Saie-Saye — Coat with cape or ordinary sleeves, front buttoned, worn with or without a belt, worn by pages designed for show in rich material.

- ◆ Sailor Suit — Constumes inspired by the uniforms of French and English sailor, adopted for boys; it has square collar, trimmed with narrow white braid.

- ◆ Samite — Silk cloth which must have been related to candal, but richer and stronger.

- ◆ Sampot — Piece of cloth which the Combodians wind around the waist and take up between their legs, draping it to form something like trousers.

- ◆ Sandal — Foot wear worn only by women adopted by certain Roman religious orders with the leather sole straped on to the foot, to protect the toes and a quarter fitting the heel.

- ◆ Sarong — Long cloth wound round the body in Malaya.

- ◆ Sayon — Some authors have defined the sayon as a Gaulish Cassock. The term donates a sleeved Cassock, belted at the waist.

- ◆ Sbernia — Outer garment worn by women. It was a sort of long scarf draped from a pin on the left shoulders.

- ◆ Scarf — Originally satchel worn over one shoulder.

♦	Segmentum	Band of cloth of gold or precious stuff used to decorate the garments of Roman women.
♦	Serapis	Long tunics of fine pleated stuff worn by Persian women.
♦	Serpentaux	Women's hairstyle, with barely curled hair hanging down.
♦	Shawl	Large rectangle of woolen or any other material which is wrapped on the body to keep it warmth.
♦	Shenti	Sort of loin cloth worn in Egypt, made of a long narrow piece of linen cloth passed between the legs. The end, folded over, forms a projecting tab above the waist enabling the wearer to tighten the garment. Pharaohs are often portrayed wearing only the shenti.
♦	Siglaton	Gold brocade originating from the east; made in Lucca used for very luxurious garment.
♦	Simarra	In Italy an outer gown whose form varies from province to province, but which was always opened over an undergown.
♦	Sindon	Egyptian cloak made of a large draped piece of linen.
♦	Skarangion	Long Persian gown, furlined and buttoned at the side.
♦	Scarabicon	Outer garment of high Byzantine dignitaries.
♦	Skiradion	Head dress worn by Byzantine dignitaries.
♦	Skull Cap	Small hemispherical cap covering the top of the head; sometimes flat or with rounded point or even with a short tail, adopted by the clergy.
♦	Slashings	Small openings made in a garment showing the lining, slashing was made in garments, shoes and gloves.
♦	Slippers	Originally called solers, this term describes footwear covering the foot.
♦	Slops	Large unpadded breeches which extended to the knees.
♦	Snood	Net used to cover the head gear, nets decorated with pearls and jewel were worn directly over the hair.
♦	Soccus	Wide ceremonial clock; open, fastened on the right shoulders, worn by king for his coronation and other major ceremonies.
		A sort of slipper or shoes without fastening completely covering the foot, worn by both sexes.
♦	Solea	The simplest form of Roman sandal a wooden sole with a cord

passing over the foot.

- ◆ Solleret — Piece of armour protecting the foot.

- ◆ Solitaire — With hair styles men generally wore a ribbon bow round the bourse behind the neck; its long ends were knotted in front of the shirt collar. The term formerly described women's neck-bows.

- ◆ Sombrero — Man's hat with the shape used for long time in Iberian Peninsula. A soft hat with or without orchid's feather, turned up the brim on the right side.

- ◆ Sorquenie — Tunic fitted tightly over the bust, worn by women. The ward was then applied to the smocks of coachmen and ostlers.

- ◆ Sottana — A tunic under garment, sometimes in plain material, sometimes in alternate, differently coloured bands of linen cloth. Young girls worn it as an outer gown.

- ◆ Soulette — A leather band that passed over the instep and under the patten, to hold it to the boot.

- ◆ Spencer — Short jacket reaching to the waist with long sleeves that covered the hand, worn mainly by women in the Directoire period.

- ◆ Steinkirk Cravat — After the battle of Steinkirk in 1692, Mile Le Rochois, a singer at the opera appeared with a lace cravat thrown over her coat and this continued in fashion.

- ◆ Stemma — Circlet set with gems and decorated with hanging ornaments, sometimes topped with a cross worn by the Byzantine emperors.

- ◆ Stephanos — Crown set by Byzantine emperors to Vassal Monarch and high dignitaries.

- ◆ Stivali — Light boots fitted close to the leg in France, high and soft, usually black, sometimes red. They are summer footwears.

- ◆ Stole — Typical garment of the Roman women, and the toga of Roman citizen, long and loose, it is worn over the chemise and fastened to the body by two belts one under the breast and one on the hips.

- ◆ Stole — A kind of scarf or a long band which the priest wears over the mict and under the chasuble.

- ◆ Strophium — Scarf wound into a long even cord and tied round the body to support the breasts. It was worn over a short tunic, unlike the mamillare, worn next to the skin.

◆ Subligaculum   Piece of cloth passed round the waist and between the thighs, fastened under the fork; it made sort of short trousers like those worn by boatsmen.

◆ Subucula   Under tunic of wool worn under the true tunic.

◆ Succinta   Wide belt worn by both sexes to grid in garments at the waist so that they could be tucked up for walking.

◆ Suffibulum   Large rectangle of white cloth worn on the head hanging down behind, fastened with a brooch under the chin; worn by vestal and priest during sacrifices.

◆ Suit   An ensemble for men, comprising jacket, waist coat and trousers in the same material, and matching frock coat and waist coat with striped trousers.

◆ Supparium   Short linen garment which Roman women wore over the subucula.

◆ Surcoat   A long over coat with or without sleeves worn over the coat often used by men for riding.

◆ Surtout   Term used for a very long time for mens cloaks and coats.

◆ Swedish hat   Large felt hat popularised by musketeer's dress worn by troops during thirty years' war of Sweden.

◆ Synthesis   A sort of tunic worn for meals by Romans.

◆ Tabard   A kind of military and a ceremonial coat with free hanging back and front and short wing sleeve.

◆ Tablion   Oblong embroidered with the image of the monarch.

◆ Tailored Coat   Introduced in 1910, a women's coat with severe English cut, always worn buttoned.

◆ Tailored Suit   Woman's costume composed of a jacket and skirt, mannish in cut.

◆ Talaris Tunic   A long sleeved, long grided tunic worn by women and elderly men.

◆ Tassel   A triangle of cloth, usually black, filling in the bodice neck line.

◆ Tassettes   Basques of the doublet.

◆ Tebenna   An Etruscan cloak, completed with a hooded cap.

◆ Templet   Metal ornament round which women's hair was rolled above the ears.

♦	Therese	A loose head-dress in a form of a hood which could be worn over the tall bonnets.
♦	Tholia	A hat with a pointed crown and flat brim worn by Greek women.
♦	Thorakion	A coat of arms (crest) of the empresses of Byzantium.
♦	Tiara	National head dress of all South-West Asiatic people, a soft crown held in place by a narrow ribbon round the head.
♦	Tibiales	High leggings worn by Roman huntsmen or soldres.
♦	Tippet	Medieval streamer hanging from the sleeve of a cothardie or a kind of short shoulder cape.
♦	Toga	Roman national costume, made up of white wool.
♦	Toga Trabea	Short Etruscan toga decorated with purple bands, royal robe adopted by Romulus and his successors.
♦	Toga Gabiana	Roman toga, tight fitting with one fold thrown over the heads and the other taken behind over the hips to form a belt.
♦	Tontillo	Farthingale with steel hoops still worn in Spain at the end of 17th century.
♦	Torque	Roman and Gallo-Roman neckline in the form of a variously ornamented circle.
♦	Tour	False hair worn on the front of the head.
♦	Touret	Women's head dress; a veil covering the fore-head, as in coifs worn by nuns.
♦	Trabea	Brocaded scarf worn by consuls of the late Roman Empire, and of the Basilean period in Byzantium.
♦	Tressoir	Golden plait of silk worked with metal and gems worn by women in 13th century.
♦	Trousers	Below waist garment worn since the earliest times by horse-riding steppe people.
♦	Trousses	Upper hose which did not hang down but fitted the thighs tightly.
♦	Troussoir	Hook designed to lift the long gowns worn by womens, also a flowing scarf hanging down one side, on which women hung their small objects.
♦	Truffau/Truffe	Some authors interpret these as false hair worn on the temples or pads used in the tall hair styles of late 14th century.

- Trunk hose — Upper hose or leg garment which extended from waist to knee.

- Tunic Ala mameluck — Reminiscent of Napoleon's Egyptian campaign: a women's tunic with half length, long or short sleeves.

- Tunic A La Romaine — Long gauze or lawn tunic with a very high waist and long sleeves of one form which was classically inspired Directoire styles.

- Turban — Eastern head dress formed of a cap round which a long piece of cloth (wool, cotton or silk) is rolled starting in the middle of a tall woolen or felt crown criss-crossing until the ends are tucked into folds. Fine red cotton stuffs are used to make turbans.

- Tutulus — Roman women's hair style, with all the hair piled up in a cone on top of the head; also a conical cap, worn in particular in some seminaries.

- Tzitsakion — Eastern garment adopted by the court of Byzantium.

- Upper Stocks — Breeches or hose which covered the lower part of the trunk as well as the upper part of the leg.

- Vair — Fur of the northern grey squirrel; it was blue grey on top and white underneath. This fur was reserved exclusively for the robes of kings or high magistrates.

- Venetians — Breeches whose bouffant shape took the form of the long oval tied at the knee by garter ribbons.

- Verdugo — Literally a rod or wand/rigid frames designed to support the fullness of gown. This developed into the farthingale.

- Vest — Mens garment worn under a coat; they are very short, often sleeveless. Generally made in rich materials.

- Vestes — Term used in Rome for the piece of woven cloth draped by the wearer.

- Vis a Giere — Open part of the hood around the face.

- Visite — Cloak in the form of large printed shawl, buttoned in front with two front slits, edged with embryonic sleeves.

- Vitta — Bandeau worn round the head to hold the hair back.

- Vlieger — Woman's garment such as ropa worn in low countries until 1640.

- Volant — Light unlined jerkin worn as a surtout, it had no pockets buttons or button holes on the sleeves or tabs, the neck was fastened with a button.

◆ Waist Coat — Waist coat was worn by men and women as an outer garment over any garment. It does not have sleeves, printed fabric is used for front and plain at back, buttoned in front (sometimes).

◆ Walking suit — Suit with a skirt barely touching the ground, it was three to four inches off the ground.

◆ Watteau Pleat — Box pleat sweeping down from the shoulders to the hem in the loose back of a gown, fitted in front and sides.

◆ Weepers — White band worn on the sleeve facing of coats and jerkins for deep mourning in 17th-18th centuries.

◆ Witchoura — Hooded, fur trimmed over coat of Polish origin, the sleeves could be left hanging wider, less stiffy, worn by young men in 1808. It re-appeared during the Romantic period.

◆ Woad — Alternative name for pastel.

◆ Zancha — Boot fitting the leg tightly and rising very high, in soft black leather. During Roman period it was worn by Eastern people under their trousers.

◆ Zona — In Greece from the 9th century BC, a broad flat belt which girls wore on the hips. It was discarded only when they are married, the husband unfastening it after the ceremony. The ordinary belt was below the breasts.

◆ Zouave Pantaloons — A wide pantaloon with the legs gathered below the knee into a tight band trimmed with a frill.

Fashion Industry

CHAPTER 11

Boutique and Its Importance

Even the leading fashion designers are the vulnerables, if their sense of direction and development is not consistently strong they will fail to develop a progressive adaptability. The stereotypical type of result could leave the way open for new designers, who have a better understanding of the way fashion develops. So it is necessary for the designers to create a brand equity of their own through a boutique and sustain it.

The role of a designer in a boutique is crucial to its success. The task is specially one of the interpreting society's current and anticipated mood into desirable, wearable garments for every type and level of market. To do this effectively, designers must be in tuned with the wider social, cultural, economics and political environment within which human beings conduct their daily lives. Only then their ideas truly reflect current prevailing conditions and the impact they are likely to have on future consumer needs.

Therefore, the designer will draw on a wealth of ideas, the media and entertainment, other cultures, social attitudes and moves, historical and contemporary events all provide important sources of inspirations. The skill in any good design really lies in maximizing the values that can be added to set the basic raw materials. It is thus dependent on the quantity of the original design, its suitable design for the market and the way it is made to meet customers requirements.

It's always better for a designer who works for a boutique to understand a sequence of events in the fashion world. There are four major stages of influence in the new product development and fashion diffusion and adoption process. These are chronologically as:

1) The colour meeting.
2) The biannual yarn and fabric fairs.
3) The biannual international fashion fairs in Paris.
4) Reportage in the trade and commercial press.

The Colour Meeting

"The Colour Meeting" in Paris is known as the concentration where approximately forty leading fashion industries representing major yarns, textile and garment manufacturers, top designers, stylists, colour consultants and fashion forecasters gathered together, they establish the major colour trends (based on 30 colours) that will dominate the fashion scene for two years from the time of their meeting. The trends will usually be based on themes of dark, bright, pastel and neutrals. Work then begins by various sections of the industry on interpreting and adopting the basic story to suit their own particular requirements. For e.g., the International Wool Secretariat and Cotton Institute will work on appropriate interpretation for their respective yarn and textile industry.

The Biannual Yarn and Fabric Fairs

Where the new colours, textures and patterns will be presented as trend for twelve months ahead. In France major fair is Premier Vision, in Germany it is called "Intersoft" and in U.K. it is called "Fabrea". Premier Vision also features an audio visual presentation, the details, the sources of ideas and inspirations used by the concertation team.

The Biannual International Fashion Fair

In Paris, Milan, New York, and London where leading designers present their latest collections and ideas six months ahead of the season in question. Representation by the media is very strong at the International Collection, showing the enormous influence the media now have on fashion awareness and acceptance.

Reportage in the Trade and Commercial Press

The designer collections—the power and extent of modern day mass communication system is such that the media is instrumental in shaping and influencing the fashion that are ultimately

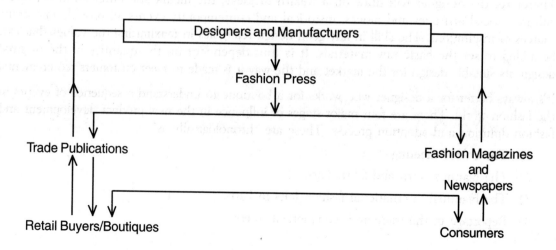

accepted. This Process is shown in the figure below. Simultaneously journalist now provide a two-way flow of information reporting 'upwards' on the street styles that have been a significant influence on top designers over the last few years (on often creating their own fashions and fads in the process), as well as downwards on developments in the collections of the public.

The garments made for the Boutiques and Mass Productions are quite different. The former evolved from the desire for luxury and conspicuous consumptions from the elite strata (high level) of the society. The latter developed in response to the growing post war affluence of the majority and the desire for an improvement in living standards and life styles. Therefore the function of mass production is to select and adopt appropriate designs from the boutiques to meet the needs of the public at large. It is necessary for a boutique owner to know the difference between fashion and fad. The distinction between the fashion and fad is usually defined on the basis of their acceptance cycle. Fashion usually has a slower rise to popularity, reach a plateau with continuing popularity and then decline gradually, often this cycle relates to season, whether autumn/winter or spring/summer. Mid season modification to the original fashions may be introduced with the specific intention of maintaining buying interest and encouraging further purchases from early as well later adoptors.

Fads on the other hand will rise meterically in popularity only to suffer the decline as they become adopted. As the Fad becomes fashionable, it also becomes unfashionable. Adopting of the Fad is based solely on the desire by the individual for a new experience that is not likely to become popular on a large scale. For this reason a fad tends to be viewed as non-viable in the commercial sense and usually eccentric in nature.

The Present Structure of the Fashion Indusry

The manufacture and sale of clothes today is one of the worlds most important industries. The structure of the fashion industry has changed as it has expanded and diversified.

Little has changed, though, with regards to the creative aspects of fashion design. The head of a collection is surrounded by the team of designers and dress makers. He is responsible for choosing the season's line and fabrics and selecting which models will be made on the premises in his work-room. Finally he chooses the establishment's models, on whom the collection will be presented to the public.

There are two collections a year, one for the spring-summer season, which is shown to buyers and the press in late January, and one for the winter, which is shown in late July. Each collections includes between fifty (minimum required) and a hundred and fifty pieces. Sales of garments made to order for a specific client, with at least two fittings, are now very rare. Instead, the industry survives by selling the working patterns that can be reproduced in a simpler versions and less expensive materials by manufacturers. The sale of designer accessories has also been increasing.

The process of industrial manufacturing is a good deal more complex than that of the design, in many cases the design house place a big part. The industry's companies vary; some are private, some financed by professional federations or sectors of the textile industry. These companies serve as liaisons between the various elements of production, including choosing colours and materials, producing a design catalogue, assembling collections meant for firm without a design team of their own, and organizing promotional publicity aimed at department stores and, above all, the mail-order houses that handle a vast amount of the clothing market. If the more daring creation of the great designers prove unacceptable to the general public, they will often consent to design a more modest collection that will sell more widely. The prestige of the label remains, even with clothes that sell for much less than those in the high-fashion line.

The schedule for production is much longer than that for design, which remains an essentially artisanal craft. Colours and fabrics are fixed, in general, two years before the sale of collection. Materials are chosen between February and April, a line is chosen in May, and then a small number of samples are made for sales representatives to test on clients. This process allows manufacturers to adjust their production needs according to the best-received models.

These pieces are presented by buyers in October for the following summer season, while winter models are shown in April. Clothes are manufactured according to demand. The summer line is ready to be delivered in April, the winter line in October.

The complex operation of the fashion industry requires exacting organisation and depends on the perfect synchronization of the suppliers and the manufacturers. The stakes are high enough to make clothes manufacturing an extremely rigorous industry. In an effort to avoid the arduous demands of the system. " Pirate" companies have sprung up to obtain the most engaging models from the salons and copy them, often using illegal labour. Their clothes are then sold to boutiques that have not managed to secure rights with the original designers.

The fashion industry enjoyed a spectacular rate of development until 1974. Then, due to the world-wide energy crisis that caused prices for raw materials and therefore retail goods to soar, the industry slowed considerably until 1980. A number of companies closed during this period. The crisis now seems to be over, and once again the fashion industry is expanding.

Textiles and Materials in the Fashion Industry

In the near future, when the production of natural fabrics will not suffice to clothe a rapidly growing population, synthetic and artificial material will become a necessity.

 Though greater discoveries are made in the field of textiles twenty or thirty years ago, researchers are learning better ways to use new materials, including mixing synthetics among themselves or with wool and cotton. The most popular synthetics remain Tergal and its derivatives, nylon and Rilsan, which brought new life to the manufacturing of undergarments and stockings and were a particularly welcome development with tights came into vogue.

As for designers, they continue to prefer the traditional textiles. It is also interesting to note that the designers use textiles intended for uses other than fashion.

The hosiery trade during this period was booming they were seen as unfashionable articles of clothing to be hidden under other garments, were being produced in mesh fabrics with printed or woven patterns for men and women. Manufactured much more quickly, and thus become more cheaper than woven fabrics, the new mesh fabric also had the advantage of being more wrinkle-resistant. The base of "fake fur" was made of mesh material. Designer had long tried to imitate real fur with synthetic materials. With the surge of ecologists campaign to protect endangered species, the trend toward fake furs rose. But many designers also fabricated whimsical variations on the real thing — fake animal skin were cheaper than originals.

This era witnessed a heightened appreciations for both real and imitation leather, which had the advantage of existing in large pieces than natural leather. Dull or shiny, leather is very much in fashion used as pants, jacket, and motor cycle suits, but also in woman's coats. The western specialists in leather clothes have been claude Montana, Azzedine Alaia, and recently Givenchy.

Finally one must mention the new unwoven fabrics that were produced through the process analogous to that of paper manufacturing and were meant for only one wearing. They were used to make surgical uniforms, jackets for airplane passengers, and uniforms for mechanics. When crimped, these fabrics could be used for beach dresses, bathing suits and underwears. Because the fibers of the material were held together by resin, new self-adhesive facings were obtained that were applied with hot iron, thus replacing the more expensive traditional methods of lining.

In the history of fashion, the years were constituted a period of reorganisation and regrouping after a decade of tumultuous experiences. The young always the most sensitive and dynamic facet of society, refused the commercialisation of their particular style by creating what was mistakenly seen as an anti-style. Rather, it was a hyper-stylisation that largely called upon the personal tastes of its followers. The designers, whose original customers had grown older, become the most significant force in the fashion world.

The magical atmosphere of the haute-couture collections of days past was now applied to a vaster, more varied fashion industry, which addressed itself to an increasingly diversified clientele. Designer's presentations were eagerly awaited each season. For it was from their collections that the "in" clothes would be chosen, allowing the initiated to set themselves apart before the styles were mass produced and sold at less expensive prices. Remember that haute couture clothes are generally ten times more expensive than even the best ready-to-wear styles.

It was in 70's that certain designers who had apprenticed in couture house made their mark by establishing, for a brief time, a group of "industrial creators" of Paris.

The first fashion-designer's district was in Paris. Some new names altered the image of fashion. The press interested in novelty began consulting various designers and heartily supporting their efforts. For the public, designers were no longer the poor relatives of the couturiers, but admired partners in the game of fashion.

Young people of both sexes, rebelling against conformity, began to set themselves apart by choosing clothes that were not mass produced. They bought second-hand clothes at markets and these diverse elements were worn together to create a non-conformist look.

It is not yet possible to ascertain the evolution of modern fashion, since it is only with a certain distance that we can clearly determine the dominant trends. The press has the habit of signaling trends that are not always in accordance with what people are actually wearing. Unless the world suffers an economic disaster, it is unlikely we will return to the days when one single style dominated fashion. For now, Western culture seems interested in clothes inspired by the traditional dress of Asia, clothes that hang loosely on the body can take on various appearances when worn with belt and pins. We will only know later whether this look is merely a passing whim.

For women who desires one of a kind clothes, but cannot make them themselves, there still exist a few artisans who create pieces that, if not unique, are produced in very limited series and will never become factory made.

While haute couture has almost disappeared in Europe, the craft is now being reborn in United States, where small firms that create one of a kind-or-limited series clothes are multiplying.

No designers can forget the golden rule that guided haute-couture until world war I. This brief summary of current movements in the world of fashion aims to portray the rich variety in design. Human beings cannot refuse to cloth themselves without loosing their identities, and it thus seems impossible that fashion will disappear in the future. Fashion may soon benefit from innumerable variations with the help of computer technology. There remain in this world many people who have never had access to fashion, and a vast and open terrain exists for designers of the future.

The Structure of the Fashion Market

Apart from technology, the reason why fashion is now available to the masses is that there are several levels at which clothing functions.

1. Haute couture house
2. Designer wear
3. Street fashion/Mass market

Haute Couture House

They are the major fashion house of the world, run by recognised, international famous designers. They show their collection at least twice a year and sell individual garment at very high cost. For these designers, the catwalk shows are essentially a publicity exercise for their garments, perfumes and accessories.

In recent years, the haute couturier have, along with established designers, tend to move towards greater brand differentiation to capitalise on their names and some have also decentralised their manufacturing operations to cut costs.

Some manufacturers now produce and distribute designer collections enabling haute-couture or designer names to be made available to a large market at more accessible prices through ready to wear ranges. The announcement by the French government in 1922 that is was planning to encourage new designers into haute couture indicated the fact that the couture market is in decline.

Younger customers are being tempted away from the idea of luxury for its own sake and are now demanding clothes by the newer designers that are indisputably contemporary in their direction and approach.

Designer Wear

Designer wear is shown at the "Pret-a-Porter." The move into ready-to-wear clothing by designer meant that they could offer their stylish designs and high quality to a wider audience, they are to be found in designer's shops, independent stores and some of the more exclusive department stores. Designs are not limited, but are still produced in limited numbers. A ready-to-wear designer has the same aim as the haute couture designer in creating flattering, attractive fashionable garments. A ready-to-wear fashions are usually less innovative and imitative than the fashions at couture level and haute couture styles. They may create a similar version of a particular outfit that was an outstanding seller a year back.

Mass Market or Street Fashion

It is a market area in which most people buy their clothes. New fashions can be seen in the high street stores very quickly. This is an area of the market, that is undergoing many changes. The three tier view of market is perhaps over simplistic as there are many strata and price levels between the ones mentioned. Many customers do not stick to any one level when buying their clothes. The more affluent will buy several haute couture outfits but turn to designer wear for everyday. Women who mostly buy designer ready-to-wear may occasionally splash out on a couture dress for a very special occasion. Those who generally only buy mass marketing clothing may still buy designer wear occasionally if only from the discounted retail outlet.

Second-hand Clothing—in some high street shopping centres charity shops seems to be almost as common as new clothing shops. Because of the huge increase in the number of these, the secondhand clothing outlets can be explained in many ways.

As people buy more new clothing, the second-hand clothing shops are an obvious place for them to dispose of their unwanted fashion from last season. Economic reasons could lead us to assume that lack of money means that the only clothing some people can afford is from the second-hand market or it could be that more environmentally conscious people are preferring to buy second hand and so recycling clothing rather than always buying new.

Fashion Promotion

Fashion Promotion has a large impact on all levels of the fashion business today. A large fashion promotion campaign can often put over a new fibre as a new fashion concept, whereas in the natural course of things new ideas may not be accepted. The industry is always searching for new and exciting ways to reach and impress the public. Promotion has its limit. It is ultimately the consumer who accepts or rejects a new fashion look. Effective communication is as important to channel members as it is to consumers, and it is promotion mix that provides the necessary tools and techniques.

Advertising, publicity, special events and display helps to promote sale in retailing. Advertising is the use of paid time or space in media such as television, radio, newspaper, magazines or direct mail. Large stores after have their own advertising department, although outside agencies may produce television or radio, commercials. No media costs are paid for publicity, but material used is the choice of the media editors. Special events such as fashion shows also attempt to promote products and store image. Display is the visual presentation of the stores merchandising message. Promotional efforts are co-ordinated with buyers in each merchandising area.

Some of the main techniques for fashion promotion are:

— Fashion Advertising

— Fashion Conferences, Trade Fairs and Exhibitions

— Fashion Journalism

— Window Display

Fashtion Advertising

Advertising is becoming more prominent as companies recognise the need to develop strong brand or corporate/boutique image not just at consumers, but at the trade as well.

A strong brand or corporate image can put companies/boutiques in a powerful position negotiating contracts with retailers.

The use of branding corporate/boutique image by fashion companies was in the notion of 'complete look'.

Advertising is used to promote a corporate/boutique image. It can be valuable tool for fostering goodwill of the Company. To be effective fashion advertising has to be noticed. In advertising, media is the general term used to cover all methods of transmitting a sales message. Advertisers must choose the medium that will best promote an event or best will reach the target market. Generally fashion advertising is visually oriented the philosophy being "WHY TELL THE WORLD IF YOU CAN SHOW IT". Decisions are made not only about which general medium will be used but also about which particular radio, television, station, newspaper or magazine will reach the appropriate customer for specific merchandise. Each consumer group has unique taste, ideas, and interests and consequently responds to different media. Advertising departments or agencies must determine the best possible combination of media to reach the particular target market.

To maintain public interest, repetition is necessary part of advertising. Consistency is equally important. The same ad read at the same time every day on radio or a fashion ad in the same illustration style every week on the same page in the newspaper makes people keenly aware of the store or brand name as well as the fashion message.

Objectives

— To increase market share

— To increase sales of specific product

— To create brand/fashion awareness

— To reassure customers.

— To launch a new product/garment.

— To encourage customer to trade up from one garment or service to a more experi ence one.

— To reinforce the corporate/boutique identity.

— To generate enthusiasm from channel-members.

— To increase store traffic.

— The main advertising media are Press, TV, Radio, Cinema, Posters, Hot Air-balloons and Direct Mail.

Fashtion Journalism

The fashion consumer is not born with the knowledge of fashion brands, criteria of judging the colour and style to buy. Fashion journalism is again involved with fashion promotion. Therefore this is a media through which the consumer acquires knowledge about the present fashion trends and colour.

Objectives

—   They let fashion consumer know about the famous brands, new and upcoming brands.

—   They help to give the knowledge about the colours, style, silhouettes and fabric that is in, at a particular given period of time.

—   Gives knowledge about national and international fashion world.

—   The comments of fashion journalists after a fashion show or trade fair can greatly influence trade buyers as well as consumers.

—   They give an editorial on a fashion company showing the growth of an organisation.

—   It gives an insight about opportunities available for budding designers.

—   It gives news about the upcoming designers and boutiques etc.

Conferences, Trade Fairs and Exhibitions

Trade fairs, exhibitions and conferences comes under the category of sales promotion. Trade fair, exhibitions and conferences are very important as they provide face to face contact with specifically targeted customers or potential customers and a high proportion of those attending have buying authority. They also have the ability to generate high quality leads for conversion to sales. It is estimated that nearly 84 percentage of exhibition visitors have a buying influence of some kind.

Fashion exhibitions are often very large, visitors tend to plan their routes carefully. Assuring they visit particular stands is a priority and makes location so important. A site that gives good viability and is likely to gain customer traffic because of its position is obviously better.

In estimating the size of space needed exhibitors should consider estimating how many visitors the company is aiming to talk to and for how long. Promotional material and displays are often used to create a particular ambience or theme symbolic of the exhibiting company or its products or services.

Use of artwork can attract attention and promote interest in the stand. The most commonly used types of promotional material at fashion exhibitions are post cards, leaflets, brochures, business cards, small posters and videos.

Fashion Shows

Fashion shows can be targeted at both consumer and the trade. Designer fashion shows are attended predominantly by trade and fashion journalists and photographers who are invited to preview the latest season's collections. The major international shows take place in Paris, London, Milan and New York and are excellent vehicles for gaining designer publicity.

Being able to create, winning designs is not enough. Designers need to promote themselves. Fashion shows can create a desirable designers name such that retail buyers may then wish to be associated with. Excluding the major designer shows, there are charity shows and retail sponsored shows which the public can attend, and through which publicity can be attained by the designer, manufacturer and retailer

Fashion Message Windows

Ways to co-ordinate accessories for the newest look, draws attention to stimulate the customer to buy a new garment and/or accessories.

Window Display

In the competitive fashion business it is very important to attract the customer to buy the garment. Going by the saying "First impression lasts long, garment manufacturers/boutiques display the garments inside windows to draw the attention of the customer. Though there is no fast and hard rule about how to display the garment behind the window glass, but care must be taken about proper arrangement effectively to catch the eyes of the customer.

Generally mannequins are kept in the windows and are draped accordingly to predefined theme and the theme is maintained throughout the display. In addition to the garments on display, the decorative accessories lighting etc. can be used to create the required environment/background to support the relevance of the theme. The theme could be ethnic, Western or contemporary etc., and can be changed from time to time to continue to draw the attention of the customer.

Windows can set a mood, convey a fashion message or directly sell merchandise.

Mood Windows

They convey the spirit of holiday or suggest the idea of gift for any occasion—a festival or birthday.

Direct Sell Windows

Used mostly by stores that carry popularly priced merchandise, show a representative assortment of the store's merchandise accompanied by prices; to tempt the customer with a possible bargain.

Visual merchandisers or window dressers, as they are called in common parlance, are today looked up as important and necessary executives. Apart from the working knowledge of design and applied arts, the other major requirement to create an interesting and effective show window are creativity, energy and imagination.

The mannequin and other props form the minor part of the total setting. These are other important areas like the main theme, the background, the colour scheme etc. to be visualised and executed.

Though the job includes ingenious placement of merchandise, designing the whole environment, and presenting the merchandise to the customers in a visually fascinating manner. They play a significant role in contributing to the sales and in attracting the customer's valuable attention.

In India, professional window dressers or visual merchandisers are few and far between. Two names however promptly comes to once mind are Perine Irani and Nazneen. Perine an extremely youthful looking lady, received her first window dressing assignment from Bombay Dyeing.

Fashion Designers and Their Famous Labels

13 CHAPTER

Adrian

After a successful career of designing for movies Gilbert Adrian, formed Adrian Ltd. in 1941, with headquarters in Beverly Hills. He retired in 1952 and thereafter briefly designed a line of men's shirts and ties.

Armani

Giorgio Armani began designing under his own name in 1974. Today, besides his top-level line, he designs both an Emporio Armani collection and a line known in Italy as Mani and in USA as Gioragio Armani.

Augusta Bernard

In 1919, Augusta Bernard opened her house in the rue Rivoli, in 1928 she moved to 3, rue du Faubourg St., Honore, where she remained in business until 1935.

Balenciaga

Balenciaga opened his house on the Avenue Georges V in 1937 where he remained until retiring in 1968 Eisa was the name of his Spanish couture houses in Madrid and Barcelona.

Balmain

Balmain opened his house at 44, rue Francois Premier in 1945. In addition to his first couture label, he has designed numerous boutique accessories and other lines. Since his death in 1982, his former right hand man, Erick Mortensen, has been the house's premier designer.

Bill Blass

After designing for the now defunct Seventh Avenue firm of Anna Milles Ltd., Bill Blass worked with Maurice Rentner in 1959. By 1960 the company's advertisements read "Bill Blass for Maurice Rentner", and by 1961 he was made a Vice President. Bill Blass Ltd., was founded in 1970.

Boue Soeurs

Mme. Sylvie Boue Montegut and the Baronne D' Etreillis (nee Boue) founded their houses in 1989 at 9, rue de la Paix, their New York branch opened around 1916 and the house stayed in business through 1931.

Bonnie Cashin

After costuming over forty Hollywood movies, Bonnie Cashin moved to New York in 1949 to try her hand at sportswear. Bonnie Cashin Ltd. was founded in 1953, and from her studio she has turned out designs for various manufacturers, most notably Phillip Sills and Ballantyne. In 1972 she established the Knittery for the manufacture of hand-knitted clothing from hand spun yarns.

Callot Soeurs

The house of Callot Soeurs at 24, rue Taitbout, was founded in 1895 by Mesdames Marie Callot Gerber, Marthe Callot Bestrand, and Regina Callot Chantrelle. In 1914 the house moved to 9-11, Avenue Matignon and it was around this time that it began dating its labels. During the 1920's Callot established branches in Nice, Biarritz, Buenos Aires, and London. By the time Mme Gerber retired in 1937, the branches had closed and the house was absorbed into another house, Calvet. Desings continued to appear bearing the Callot label, however, until Calvet closed in 1948.

Chanel

Chanel began her hat business in 1908 in a basement apartment at 160, Boulevard Malesherbes. In 1912 she moved to 21, rue Cambon. Her houses in Deauville and Biarritz were opened in 1913 and 1916 respectively. In 1928 she moved into three floors of 31, rue Cambon, closing the house from 1939-54. Following her death in 1971, her assistants Yvonne Dudel and Jean Cazaubon tookover designing the couture, with Phillippe Guibourge in charge of the Chanel Boutique, launched in 1976. Accessories have been designed by Frances Stein since 1981, and in 1984, Karl Lagerfeld formally and officially tookover as designer of both couture and ready to wear.

Courreges

After working for Balenciga for ten years, Andre Courreges opened his house in 1961 at 48 Avenue Kleber. 1965 he relocated to 40, rue Francois Premier and inaugurated his system of fashion levels. Prototypes is the Label for the haute couture and Couture Future the deluxe ready to-wear. In 1970 he added another tier, Hyperbole, for younger clients and budgets.

Charles James

Charles James started his career in 1924 in Chicago as a milliner using the name of Boucheron.

He began designing clothes and headed to London via New York, where he spent most of the 1930s designing clothing under versions of his own name at various addresses, occasionally showing in Paris. Just before world war II he returned to New York, where he intiated multiple businesses over the years until retiring as an active designer in 1958. He died in 1978.

Claire McCardell

McCardell worked as a knitwear designer before becoming assistant to designer Robert Turk, accompanying him to the firm of Townley, where she remained for eight years until the firms 1938 closing. A stint at Hattie Carnegie followed Townley reopened in January 1941, and McCardell emerged as the main designer, with her name on the label, and she remained there-becoming a Vice President and partner in 1952 until her death in 1958.

Dior

Christian Dior worked for both Robert Piguet and Lucien Lelong before opening his own house in 1947 at 30, Avenue Montaigne. In 1953 he hired the young Yves Saint Laurant, who by 1955 was designing for the house and, upon Dior's death in 1957, was chosen to succeed him. Marc Bohan became the house couturier in 1960. Ready-to-wear was designed by Philippe Guibourge during the 1970's and by Gerard Penneroux beginning in 1983. Christian Dior-New york began in 1949, and the London operation in 1955. Baby dior was born in 1969; Miss Dior in 1966.

Doucet

When Jacques Doucet established his Maison de Couture in 1871, it was a division of a house established over fifty years earlier by his grand-mother as a lace shop on the Boulevard Saint-Martin. The house had moved in 1837 to 17 rue de La Paix and had been divided by Edouard Docet in 1869 into two adjoining shops, a chemisier for men and a ladies shop for lace and lace-trimmed lingerie.

The couture house of Doucet was located next door at 21, rue de La Paix. Poiret worked there as a designer from 1897 to 1900 as did Vionnet (around 1903 to 1908). Jacques Doucet died in 1929 and his house merged to form Doveillet Doucet, which lasted until 1932.

Fortuny

Mariano Fortuny made his first garment in 1906, stencilled silk knossos scarves for a Paris ballet performance. The following year he created his first pleated Delphos dress, patenting the process in 1909. By 1912 he was producing a large variety of stencilled velvet robes, cloaks, dresses, wall hangings, and cushions at his Pallazzo Orfei in Venice, and displaying them in a Paris shop at 2, rue de Marignon and one in London at 29 Maddox Street. By 1924 he had moved his Paris location to 67, rue Pierre Charron. After his death in 1949, the Contessa Gozzi, an associate and owner of the Fortuny shop at 509 Madison Avenue in New York, tookover management of the Fortuny factory in Venice. Production of the pleated dresses halted in 1953 and Fortuny today produces only the stencilled cotton furnishing materials.

Geoffrey Beene

Geoffrey Beene designed for Harmaj, the Seventh Avenue Firm, from 1950 to 1957, his name sometimes featured in ads for the house. At Traina, Inc., where he next worked, his name appeared on the company label. He started designing for himself in 1962, opening Geoffrey Beene, Inc., on Seventh Avenue. Since then his label has appeared on an ever growing number of lines.

Galanos

James Galanos worked for Hattie Carnegie in New York, Robert Piguet in Paris, and Daidow back in New York before moving to Los Angeles and founding his own business in 1951. Since 1953 he has been showing his california-designed-and-made collections in New York.

Gallena

Maria Monaci Gallena was an artist who began making clothes in 1914, showing them in Rome and in Florence, where her studio was located in the Viade' Tornabuoni. She frequently incorporated her signature into the pattern her materials. By the twenties she sometimes also used a printed label.

Givenchy

Hubert de Givenchy worked for Jacques Fath, Robert Piguet, Lucien Lelong, and Schiaparelli before opening his own house in the Avenue Alfred-de Vigny in 1952. In 1957 he relocated to his present address of 3, Avenue Georges V.

Gres

Bron Germaine Barton, Gres briefly worked for the house of Premet before designing under a version of her own name, Alix Barton, at 8, rue Miromesnil. In 1934 she moved to 83, rue du Faubourg St-Honore, where she was the head designer at Alix until 1940. She opened her own house in 1942 adopting her husbands painting name of Gres- at 1, rue de La Paix, her present location. Her first Pret-a-Porter collection was shown in Spring 1985.

Hardy Amies

Amies began designing under his own name in 1941. After the war he opened his house at 14, Savile Row, where his house is today. His design partner is Ken Fleetwood.

Halston

Halston trained briefly with Charles James and with the Miliner Lilly Dache before becoming the custom hat designer at New York's Bergdorf Goodman in 1958. He branched out from Millinery when Bergdorf's gave him his own boutique in 1966. Halston Ltd. was founded in 1968 at 813

Madison Avenue, where his designs took up several floors, the couture at the top, then moved to the Olympic Towers in 1978.

Heim

The house of Heim was established by Isidore and Jeanne Heim in 1898 at 48, rue Lafitte. Jacques Heim began designing couture for his parents house in 1923 and the house moved in 1934 to 50, Avenue Matignon, and again in the 1950's to 15, Avenue Matignon. Heim Jeunes Filles, specializing in wedding dresses, was begun in 1937, and Pret-a-Porter activities, under the label Heim Actualite, started in the early 1950's. Jacques Heim retired in 1967, succeeded by his son Phillippe, who is the present Director.

Issey Miyake

Miyake studied art and design in Japan before working in Paris for Gay La Roche and Givenchy, and in New york for Geoffrey Beene. He established Miyake Design Studio in Japan in 1970.

Jean Desses

Jean Desses worked for the couture house Jane is in the rue de la Paix beginning in 1925. In 1937 he opened his own house at 37, Avenue Georges V, moving in 1948 into the mansion formerly owned by the Eiffel family at 17, Avenue Matignon. From 1958 until his retirement in 1963. He was located at No. 12 Rond-Point-des-Champs-Elysees. In 1955 he inaugurated both a Pret-a-Porter line known as diffusions and a boutique in Athens.

Jacques Fath

Jacques Fath opened his first couture house in 1937 at 32, rue de La Boetie, moving in 1940 to rue Francois Premier and in 1944 to Avenue Pierre Premier de Serbie. He opened a New York boutique in 1951 and, beginning about 1950 designed ready-to-wear collections for Joseph Halpert that were sold all over the United States. In 1954 he initiated a line for young women called Fath Universite. After his death that same year, his wife, Genevieve, operated the house until its closing in 1957.

Jacques Griffe

After working for a tailor in Toulouse, then in Paris for the House of Vionnet, Jacques Griffe opened his own house in the rue Gaillon in 1942. In 1946 he moved to 29, rue du Faubourg St-Honore, moving again to take over Molyneux's establishment at 5, rue Royale in 1950. His boutique line was called Jacques Griffe Evolution and he also designed Griffe Pret-a-Porter. He retired in 1974.

Jean Patou

Patou launched several businesses before opening a couture house under his own name. He began in 1910 with a fur and dress making establishment, switching in 1911 to a tailoring one. In 1912 he initiated Maison Parry, his first success. He had acquired the hotel particulier at 7, rue St. Florentin (where Patou remains today), just before world war I, but was not able to open officially until 1919. In 1924 he opened branches in Deauville and Biarritz followed by one in Monte Carlo. After his death in 1936, the house continued to be run by Raymond Barbas, husband of Patou's sister Madeleine and grand father of the present president, Jean de-monty. Marc Bohan and Gerard Pipart were hired as designers in 1953; Karl Lagerfeld in 1960, Michel Gona in 1963, and Angelo Tarlazzi in 1973. Christian La Croix, the Couturier there today, has been with the house since 1980.

Kenzo

Kenzo leased his first Paris shop in 1969, opening in 1970 at the Passage Choiseul and moving in 1972 to the rue Grenelle. Since 1976 his headquarters have been located at 3, Place des Victories and although, the company name is still Jungle JAP, the label has been known in America as Kenzo since 1976.

Karl Lagerfeld

Karl Lagerfeld worked for the houses of Patou and Balmain before becoming the designer at Chloe, a deluxe Pret-a-Porter house, in 1964. During his twenty years there he freelanced for several other houses, including Fendi, where he has designed furs and clothes since 1972. In 1983 he began designing couture for the house of Chenel, and has since begun designing Pret-a-Porter there too. In 1984 he ended his connection with Chloe and presented the first collection under his own label Lagerfeld.

Lanvin

Jeanne Lanvin founded her house in 1980 as a millinery business at 22, rue du Faubourg St-Honore, the same building in which the house thrives, today. She had expanded into designing ladies' and children's clothing by 1900, and by 1926 had opened, across the street, Lanvin Tailleur for men, where she also conducted a shop for sports clothes. In 1929 she initiated a fur branch on the Rond-Point-des-champs-Elysees. After her death in 1946, her daughter, the Comtesse de Polignac, took over the design direction, hiring Antonio del Castillo in 1950 as the houses couturier. When the Comtesse died in 1958, the house was bequeathed to Yves Lanvin, nephew of Jeanne and father of Bernard Lanvin, the present director. Castillo left in 1963 and was replaced by Jules Francois Crahay as couturier. In 1982, Bernard's wife Maryll Lanvin began designing Pret-a-Porter for the house, and since the 1984 retirement of Crahay has taken on more and more of the design responsibilities.

Liberty & Co.

In 1875, Arthur Lasenby Liberty founded his emporium in London, selling Oriental imports of great variety. Shortly thereafter, Liberty's began dyeing imported fabrics, then moving into the production and printing of its own fabrics. The costume department opened in 1884 under Costume Historian. Its output of clothing based on classical and artistic dress was also sold in the Paris Liberty's founded in 1890 at 38, Avenue de L'Opera. The Paris branch moved in 1920's to the Boulevard des Capucines, but closed in 1932, the same year of Paul Poirets brief affiliation with the firm. For the past fifty years, Liberty's has operated much as it first did, as a kind of electric department stores.

Louise Boulanger

Louise Boulanger worked as designer for the house of Cheruit before opening her own in 1923 at 3, rue de Berri. In 1933 the house closed briefly, with Louis Boulanger designing for Callot Soeurs before relocating her house at 6, rue Royale. The house closed in 1939.

Lucile

The then Mrs. Wallace started a dress making establishment in London's Davies Street in 1890. In 1894 she changed her business's name to Maison Lucile and moved to Old Burlington Street. She next moved to 17 Honover Square, 14 Georges Street (1898-1900), and finally to 23 Honover Square in 1900, the year she married Sir Cosmo Duff Gordon. Lucile Ltd. was formed in 1903. In 1910 she opened a New York branch at 17 West 36th Street, in 1911 a Paris branch at 11, rue de Penthieveres, and in 1913 moved the New York House to 37-39 West 57th Street, and opened a Chicago one at 1400 Lake Shore Drive. In 1918 she sold the London house, closed the Chicago one, and reopened the Paris branch. In 1924 she moved to the New York House to East 54th Street and in 1930 she went into semi-retirement, announcing she would only design for a limited clientele. She died in 1935.

Mary McFadden

McFadden was working as a special projects editor at Vogue in New York when the clothes she had designed for herself attracted notice. She began having them made up for small orders, some of which Bendel's bought, and in 1973 she went into business. Mary Mcfadden Inc. was formed in 1976.

Main Bocher

Main Bocher opened his couture house in Paris in 1930 at 12, Avenue Georges V when he closed it in 1940, he relocated to New York, opening a house at 6 East 57th Street. In 1960 he moved his house to 609 Fifth Avenue where it existed until his 1971 retirement.

Molyneux

Edword Molyneux worked for Lucile in England before opening a Maison de Couture in Paris in 1919 at 14, rue Royale. By 1921 he had moved to 5, rue Royale where his house would remain until December 31, 1950. His Monte Carlo branch opened in 1925, one in Cannes in 1927, and a London one in 1932. During World War II his business was inoperative. In 1965 he came out of retirement to begin Studio Molyneux, a Pret-a-Porter concern. He died in 1974.

Marcel Rochas

Marcel Rochas opened his couture house in Paris in 1925 at 100, rue du Faubourg St-Honore, on the place Beauvau. He moved in 1931 to 14, Avenue Matignon and in 1937 opened a New York house at 32 East 67th Street. Since his death in 1954 the house has continued to produce perfumes and accessories. Today it is located at 33, rue Francois Premier.

Maggy Rouff

Maggy Rouff opened in 1929 at 136, Avenue des Champs Elysees, where the house remained until the couturier's retirement in 1948. Then, with her daughter as designer, it moved to Avenue Matignon where it remained until 1960. Between 1960 and 1966, with designer's Jean Marie Armand and Serge Matta, the address was on the Avenue Marceau. In 1966 the house moved a last time to 14, Avenue Montaigne with Guy Douvier as the designer. Maggy Rouff died in 1971.

Norman Hartnell

Norman Hartnell Ltd., opened at 26 Burton Street in London in 1924. Briefly in the late twenties, the house showed in a Paris branch on the rue de Ponthieu. Sir Norman Hartnell designed ready-to-wear for various manufacturers before beginning with in his own in 1963. He died in 1979.

Norma Kamali

Together with her husband, Eddie, Norma Kamali opened a boutique on East 53rd Street in New York in 1968, where she sold her own designs as well as those of other designers. The boutique moved to Mansion Avenue in 1974. When she divorced her husband, she started OMC, at 6 West 56th Street, moving across the street in 1984 to number 11.

Norell

Norma Norell studied fashion illustration and worked as a movie costumer before beginning to design fashion for Charles Armour in 1924, and Hattie Carnegie in 1928. He remained at Carnegei's until 1940 when he moved to the firm of Traina, where he was offered a salary cut in exchange for having his name on the label. In 1960 Traina retired and Norell presented his first collection under his own name, continuing to do so until his death in 1972. Gustave Tassell designed for Norell until 1978.

Nina Ricci

Nina Ricci, with her son Robert, founded her house in Paris in 1932 at 22, rue des Capucines. During the fifties, Madame Ricci became more involved with overseeing general management and less with actual designing, hiring Jules Francois Crahay in 1954 as couturier. Since 1963 the house designer has been Gerard Pipart. Madame Ricci died in 1970, and was succeeded by her son, who moved his house to its present location at 33, Avenue Montaigne.

Oscar de La Renta

Oscar de la Renta worked in Balenciaga's Eisa Atelier in Mardid and in Paris for Antonio del Castillo before becoming a designer at Elizabeth Arden, New York, where his designs appeared as "by Oscar de La Renta for Elizabeth Arden". In 1965 after two years there, he began designing for Jane Derby, and it wasn't long before his name appeared alone on the label. Since Derby's death, the company has been known as Oscar de La Renta.

Pierre Cardin

After working at the houses of Paquin, Schiaparelli and Dior, Pierre Cardin founded his own house in 1950 in the rue Richepause, presenting his first collection in 1953. His boutique, Eye, opened in 1954 at 118, rue de Faubourg St-Honore, followed by Adam in 1957. In 1959 he established both man's couture line and a Pret-a-Porter line for women. Since then his boutiques, labels, and locations around the world have been countless.

Perry Ellis

Perry Ellis worked as a department store sportswear buyer before joining John Meyer of Norwich as a design director in 1968. From there he went to Vera Companies in 1974, designing a line for them in 1975 with his own label, Portfolio. Perry Ellis sportswear, Inc. was launched in 1978. In 1985 Perry Ellis revived the lesser priced Portfolio line and in addition, began to design an America line for Levi Strauss.

Paquin

Paquin opened in Paris in 1890 at 3, rue de La Paix and in 1896, Paquin London, at 39 Dover Street, became the fisrt foreign branch of a French couture house. During the twenties, Paquin had branches in Buenos Aires, Mardid, and New York, the last known as Paquin Joire. By the thirties, Paquin was under the direction of Madame del Pombo, and by the end of world war II the Paris Paquin had been emerged with the London Paquin and Worth, sharing the Paris Worth address of 120, rue du Faubourg St-Honore and its London location at 50 Grosvenor Street. Although Paquin closed in 1956, Worth was bought and sold again.

Poiret

Paul Poiret worked as a designer for the houses of Doucet (1897-1900) and Worth (1901-1904) before opening his own at 5, rue Auber in 1904. He relocated at 26, Avenue d' Antin in 1909. His school Martine was founded in 1911 and its output of furnishing fabrics and funiture was sold in its own shop. In 1925 he moved to 1, Rond-Point-des-Champs-Elysees, where he remained until being closed down by his backers in 1929. He began a new house, called Passy 10-17 in 1931 which lasted barely six months. He worked last as a designer for Liberty's but only briefly during 1932. He died in 1944.

Pauline Trigere

Pauline Trigere had worked at various fashion companies before introducing a collection of about a dozen pieces of her own in 1942. The new Company at 18 East 53rd Street, was managed by her brother, Robert. Trigere moved twice to East 47th and West 57th Streets before setting at 550 Seventh Avenue, its present headquarters.

Roberto Capucci

Capucci opened his first sartoria in Rome in 1950. Ten years later he moved to Paris, to the rue Cambon, where he remained for six years. Back in Rome in 1966, he established his house in the Via Gregoriano, where it remains today.

Ralph Lauren

Polo began as a line of men's neckties, Lauren designed for Beau Brummel in 1967. It rapidly expanded into a complete collection of mens clothing in 1968 with the addition of women's shirts in 1971, and women's separates in 1972. Since then Ralph Lauren has brought out lines of rough wear, boy's wear and girl's wear.

Sonia Rykiel

Sonia Rykiel began designing sweaters in 1963, which she sold in conjunction with her husband's Paris boutique, Laure. She opened her own boutique in 1968 at 6, rue de Grenelle, and since then has opened others allover the world.

Schiaparelli

Elsa Schiaparelli began designing, out of an upper-floor apartment at 4, rue de la Paix in 1927, with a line of sweaters. By 1930 she was able to move to a ground floor space in the same building where she offered designs "Pour le-sport" she moved to 21, Place Vendome in 1934-the same year she opened a London branch at 36 Upper Grosvenor Street. Closed during part of the war, she reopened in 1945 and continued her couture and boutique collection until 1954, when she quit the couture for good. Until her death in 1971, she designed for various licensing arrangements: Lunettes, wigs, stockings, jewelry, Swimwear, and some clothing. Schiaparelli, on the place Vendome, still dispenses perfumes as well as Pret-a-Porter and boutique items.

Vera Maxwell

Vera Maxwell began designing around 1930, working during the thirties for several sportwear, firms: Adler and Adler, Maz Millstein, and Glenhunt. She opened Vera Maxwell Originals in 1947, maintaining the firm, except for a 1964-1970 "fallow" period, until her retirement in 1985.

Valentina

In 1928 Valentina Schlee opened Valentina Gowns Incorporated at 145 West 30th Street, then moved into a town house at 27 East 67th Street in the 1940s. She retired in 1957.

Yves Saint Laurent

In 1957, Yves Saint Laurent was chosen as head designer for the House of Christian Dior, where he had worked as an assistant designer since 1953. After leaving for his military duty in 1959, and returning to find post filled by Marc Bohan, he set about opening his own house, which he did in 1962 in the rue Spontini. His first ready-to-wear boutique was opened in 1966 and his maison de couture moved in 1974 to 75 Avenue Marceau.

Zandra Rhodes

Zandra Rhodes started out in London designing fabrics for a print works set up by her and a partner. She then began designing clothes made of materials she designed. These were sold through another organisation—the Fulham Road Clothes Shop—created by her and several partners. By 1969 she was on her own and since 1975 has operated Zandra Rhodes Limited, with headquarters in London.

Valentino

Valentino Geravani worked in Paris for the couturiers Jean Desses and Guy La Roche before returning to Italy and opening his own couture house in Rome's Via Condotti in 1959. In 1967 he moved into Via Gregoriana, his present headquarters, and in 1969 he inaugurated is Pret-a-Porter, which was to be the first of many other lines.

Vionnet

Madeleine Vionnet worked for the Paris houses of Vincent, Bechoff David, Callot Soeurs, and Doucet, and for the London house of Kate Reilly before opening her own Paris establishment in 1912 at 222, rue de Rivoli. She closed during World War I and reopened in 1919, moving in until closing permanently in 1940. During 1924 she advertised a New York office at 657-659 Fifth Avenue and in 1925 a Biarritz branch in the Rotonde de Casino.

Worth

The House of Worth St. Bobergh was founded in 1858 at 7, rue de La Paix by Otto Bobergh and Charles Fredrick Worth. When Bobergh left the firm in 1870, Worth continued alone. After his death in 1895 the business was continued by his sons; Gaston Worth as business manager, Jean Phillipe Worth as couturier. From 1901-1904 Paul Poiret was a designer. In 1911 the London branch opened at 4 New Burlington Street, moving to 3 Hanover Square in 1922. By 1922 Gaston Worth had died, and the business was continued by his two sons with Jacques Worth as financial director and Jean Charles Worth as couturier. During the 1920s Worth maintained branches in Cannes and Biarritz and by 1930 there was another London location at 221 Regent Street. In 1936 the Paris house moved to 120, rue de Faubourg St-Honore, and Jacques Worth son Gaston became the couturier. At the end of World War II the Paris Worth had been merged into the Paris House of Paquin and joined with the London Worth and Paquin, now at 50 Grosvenor Street. In 1956 this combined house closed but in 1968 Worth was sold again.

INTERNATIONAL DESIGNERS VIEW OF WELL DRESSING

Being well-dressed is a subject unto itself. Whether it is fashion or not? Trendy? Inconspicuous? Emphasise? Good looking? or whether it is personal, even eccentric; style has nothing to do with the actual clothes the man is wearing?

Since fashion is a chameleon like creature, fashion's creators have their differently-shaded points of view.

Bill Blass

"Being well-dressed has to do with appropriateness, and that is why the cowboy is the best-dressed man in our country, U.S.A".

Pierre Cardin

"Todays fashion is coming out of comfort. Still, there must be shape. Shaped clothing is always more flattering to the physique, as opposed to mere body covering that some one puts on only because it's big enough to button".

Sal Casarani

Viewed as "whatever anyone wears automatically has a sense of style; the clothes say, 'this is who I am, this is what I represent'. When men buy my clothes, they are not buying my image of them; they are buying an appearance for themselves in their own Image. An image is very necessary for every individual, and basically that's what is being well-dressed is about. The other term for image is style".

Allan Flusser

"In English tailoring, to be able to spot some one's suit down street is an anathema. Really standing out in the crowd vulgarizes the concept of dressing well".

Luciano Franzoni

"What's most important is not to look phony. When every aspect is too carefully put together, a man looks unreal. Dressing well should be fun, not hard lobour. I dislike anything that smacks of putting a man in a slot, a uniform. Dressing well is being an individual".

Alexander Julian

"People with a great deal of personal style can appear well-dressed by virtue of the ease with which they display their clothing. Generally, a well-dressed man never looks out of place, as opposed to most people who consider themselves well-dressed when they are really over-dressed. A three-piece suit at a picnic looks out of place as does a bathing suit with a tie at the opening of an opera".

Bill Kaiserman

"Certain people have presence. I've seen people who at the base are not overly well-built but who look absolutely fabulous in fashion and I've seen some perfectly-proportioned models not look so great in fashion. Presentation makes the difference. Personal style has to do with feeling absolutely one-hundred percent comfortable. If someone is comfortable in what he's wearing, you look because it's one, the person and the clothing, never two. You don't judge the person naked and then the person with clothes. The clothing is person. It someone is not comfortable with the way he is dressed at any particular moment, then he is not well-dressed. If he doesn't believe in how he looks, that doubt comes through to others and he looks dishonest, a fool".

Ronald Kolodzie

"Al men live fashion, whether they realize it or not. Forget those people who say, 'oh, you look awful'. If the people you want to attract think you're sexy and are turned on, then you just keep going on the route you've chosen".

Ralph Lauren

"The well-dressed man knows who he is and dressed to express what he stands for. When he gets up in the morning, a guy thinks he's an Ivy Leaguer, a Western cowboy, a Rock star, whatever, and then he fills himself into that image at that particular time".

Don Sayres

"As with anything else, in dressing well the most important awareness is timing. No changes in clothes or fashion should completely overthrow you as a person and the way you have been dressing. On the other hand, I detest dressing in a way that hangs out a shingle and says, 'I am an art director or a doctor or whatever.' No one has to dress according to other's expectation".

Robert Stock

"Looking good is an attitude. It's how you carry it off. Being well-dressed? Realizing where the game is at and then if you want to play it but necessarily buy it. Then you know you're doing it as a fun trip, you're not taking it so seriously, and then you come off very, very strong. Attitude".

Egon Von Furtenberg

"There is a way of dressing for each age. If you stick to it, you always look the best. If you try to play the another role, you look the worst. If a man is fifty and puts on a flower-printed shirt with a pair of jeans with studs, he's going to look the worst. The better way it to wear things as simple as possible, just wearing good quality clothes".

FUTURE FASHIONS—DESIGNERS, ANALYTICAL VIEWS

Pierre Cardin

"You have to stock the eye in order to open it." This statement exemplifies Pierre Cardin's work. He is in himself, a contradiction; extravagant in his designs, conversative in his own life style. His designs are accurately labeled as "Progressively classic" and "Geometrically soft". His designs shape the fabric into fluid line retain a tight and sometimes severe silhouette. He was born lucky. In his early days as an apprentice, a fortune teller told him, "I see a growing success; I see your written in all countries of the world." With an excellent combination of his luck, backed by his amazing tenacity and latent have proved the above words true. As the originator of the bubble dress and creator of "tubes" inspired by Mondrain Paintings, Cardin has also launced women into astronaut-style space suits. Paris felt future shock and accepted the arrival of the space age.

Lynn Bowling

Lynn Bowling began his career as an architect but left that field in early 1970s, it was a time of no expansion, and work was at a standstill. The natural progression for Bouling was from housing a group of bodies to housing a single body. It's the same concept on a different scale, and he still utilizes combination of colour, shape and form. His graphics for the body focus on the use of colour; in his architectural designs, they were primarily based on shape. His understanding of shape and volume gives him an accurate eye and a precision that allows him to make a garment that is exact in its proportion and design. He prefers to work with a few colours and to alternate among few patterns and few textures. To him the challenge will be created the same excitement using less.

Bill Tice

Bill Tice believes that in the future there will be new man-made fibres and that will find new ways and new processes for working with natural ones. Man-made fibres will soon become the norm. However, natural fibres are healthier and feel better against the body, since according to Tice, they do not inhibit the electromagnetic force surrounding the body. Bill Tice has been using "colours as medicines." He believes that it has a healing force that is now being researched. Nature itself has the ability to heal, partly through its use of the most beautiful colours in the world. Our cities' gray colour can be very depressing, that is why it is so important to go to the park or to the country and replenish your energy with the colours of nature, flowers, strawberry and tree's green is the colour of life, pink is the colour of love. Yellow has a very clearing effect for the head, blue is calming, orange is energizing, and white is the most positive colour of all. If you wear white, you will attract people to you. Great ancient dresses were always in white, white bring energy to you. "If you are 'under", you may need to wear red shirt. Purple is very spiritual, very ethereal, very regal. He loves purple. When you enter a dark room, which contains great amounts of negativity, and you project a white aura, there is no question that you will suck some negativity out of the room and will make things happen in more positive way. Bad vibrations produce negative results. You might be extremely tired after you have taken the negativity with you after you leave dark room. It is possible to photograph your "colour aura". In the future people will learn to use colours.

Judyth Van Amringe for Revillon

Judyth Van Amringe designs for a special group rather than for the masses. She is an artist, and each of her pieces is like a fine drawing—an original. She sells art, not fashion. Judyth Van Amringe believes that we will soon look to romanticism for inspiration; more attention will be given to detail and to organic, natural colours. Seam will be beautifully finished so that garments will be reversible. Seams will function as part of the overall design, not just as 'endings'. Fabrics will be pieced together with new types of fastenings, which will be as beautiful as the fabrics themselves. Good workmanship, quality, textures, and sheen are all to be found in each of Judyth Van Amringe's creations.

Larry Le Gaspi

Le Gapsi finds himself working in a romantic direction, but his designs still retain structure. He feels that his work was unique eight or nine years ago, but with so many similar designs on the market, he is now forced to take a different approach. Great changes will not take place in fashion itself, according to Larry le Gaspi. Rather, new fibres and technical developments will be making the big fashion headlines, as fashion develops as part of solar energy in our clothing. Le Gaspi always works with classic elements, to which he adds futuristic flair. He believes that iridescent fabrics will be around for quite sometime. The fabrics that will become technologically important will contain metal fibres. Fabrics similar to those now used for evening wear will be used for functional designs in the future. In fifty years, according to Le Gaspi, there will be no such things as a natural fibre, unless it can be grown at the space stations. In twenty years, a silk blouse will be sold for a few thousand dollars. Land that is currently used for bleaching silk worms and growing cotton will be used for growing food. "There is only so much room here and we are multiplying by leaps and bounds every year." He believes that will use only synthetics, but the method of their production will change.

Thierry Mugler

"The prophet of futurism", as he has referred to, Thierry Mugler is an instinctive designes who never looks for inspiration. According to Mugler, "Intellect is the servant of the spirit". He strongly feels that his clothing is modernistic, not futuristic. Clothes of today should have nothing to do with the past. They should create elegance with simple form and structure and add defined shape to the body, volume, form with simplicity. "Fashion will change dramatically in the coming years. One will find less and less important to be "fashionable" ! Good design garments and well made for the purpose of protecting the body and enhancing the personality will prevail. Fashion will be mere human closer to the needs of the people in terms of their well-being and well-feeling, not well-showing". This is the direction in which he is now working.

Paco Rabanne

It was purely by accident that Paco Rabanne became a couturier. To help finance his studies in early 1960s, he created accessories for Parsian couture houses. In 1965, promoted by a sense of fashion and as a gesture of rebellion, Paco Rabanne created twelve "contemporary" dresses, which he called "The unwearables". They were composed of plastic and aluminium. The next day, Paco Rabanne was acclaimed as a couturier.

In his opinion, it is not the couturier who dictates fashion. "The couturier must be a person of immense respective powers; he must feel the needs of the world in which he lives and creates accordingly". Throughout history, there had been strong parallels between fashion and the events of the day. By looking at clothes, the keen observer may accurately predict the times ahead; long skirts appear when times are difficult; short skirts correspond to periods of affluence. Tight belts announce puritanical tendencies and attitudes; high hair styles are in fashion when regimes are about to collapse.

"Clothes symbolize an era because they concertize everything".

Paco Rabanne predicts that the clothes of the future will be premolded, bound or welded — no longer will they be sewn. "Sewing is a bondage", he says. He believes that we are in an ages of free expression and that clothes of tomorrow will be "free" — far more individual in both shape and colour. He regards today's conventional clothes as forms of punishment, and his selection for different material comes from his passionate desire to expand people's vision. He sees woman as an entirely free being. He does not wish to make her a prisoner of clothes.

Maria da Conceicao

Maria da Conceicao defines her collection of "Wearable art" in terms of adaptability, integrity, strength, and spirituality. Maria da Conceicao chooses black to represent herself; "Black is spiritual and we are going back to spirituality." Her garments are extremely versatile; they can be worn for many different occasions and continue to make the wearer feel special for an endless number of times. By adding a new layer to attain a new look, an old dress can be worn once again. "One can have a complete wardrobe with less clutter—"a simplification of life". "Pentimento," rarely used as a fashion term, accurately describes many of da Conceicao's creations. She takes a garment and overlays new fabric, lace and appliques, sometimes allowing a bit of the original fabric to peek through and thus add a touch of mystery. This Portuguese-born designer mostly enjoys working with pure cotton and pure silk. She feels that in the future there will be more natural fabrics and fewer synthetics. There will be more sheep in the fields, more cotton plantations, more worms for silk, according to da Conceicao. Making polyester fabric will contaminate the atmosphere, and therefore production will be reduced. Her Veils will protect the skin and hair from the effects of pollution.

Michael Southgate for Adel Roostein Mannequins

For the year 2002, Michael Southgate feels that fashion will become more active and more athletic in feeling, for the simple reason that people will be more body-conscious. People will eventually have better shapes; they are already becoming taller, broader and more shapely, as well as much more athletic-looking. Clothes of the future will accentuate body shapes and not cover the body, as they have done in the past and are doing at the present time. Synthetic materials work well as "clingy fashion" and future progress will continually improve the quality. The wearability of synthetics is much more practical as compared with natural fibres. Fabrics that can be molded will be developed, accordingly to Michael Southgate. In our time, spandex has been a big break-through. Wigs, too, will become an important part of fashion, especially the synthetic ones, which have a stiffer quality and can be cut into more dramatic shapes. Black is a colour that is due for a revival. We will see a good deal of it in the future designs.

Michael Southgate foresees the use of a wonderful new plastic that will be "prismatic like a rainbow, crystalline, but strong as steel, so it will never wearout."

John Anthony

John Anthony thinks that styles are borrowed from the past, although they never revert to their original form. More innovation in design will come when fashion is paired down to seperate and fewer parts; a pair of pants, a classic double-breasted jacket, or perfect sweater.

John Anthony is now working on a collection of unlined clothes; "Unlined in the sense that it is as clean on the inside as it is on the outside, without seams". Expediency in construction, the demand for finer quality, and the age of simplification determine the direction of the John Anthony collection. "The use of Zippers is outmoded." Anthony points to a photograph of a sleek model wearing one of his draped dresses, the entire dress is fastened by one hook. "Today the American way of thinking is blue jeans, cleavage and sex; a new attitude, a sexually free society. The more uniform the garment, the better". In his opinion, jeans are a good example of a more conforming attitude towards fashion. He explains that fancy clothes with frills and layers are like costumes. You cannot really wear them.

Christian Dior

On February 12, 1947, Chritian Dior presented his first collection. It was an immediate world-wide triumph. The American Press dubbed it the "New Look".

Christian Dior died ten years later. In November 1960 the haute couture collections and artistic direction of the company were placed in the hands of Marc Bohan. Bohan is not only creator but also a coordinator and a careful observer of the evolution of aesthetic trends.

Twice a year, a hundred or so new styles are created by Marc Bohan. In the choice of both colour and line, these collections, created in exclusive fabrics in a constantly renewed image, express a desire for continuity.

For a creative fashion designer the haute couture provides the finest, most glamorous, and most complete mode of expression; it is truly a laboratory and testing ground, permitting maximum research on fabrics and new silhouettes under the most favourable conditions for a satisfactory creative effort.

Insisting on quality, Bohan's creative vitality is evident in accessories, where constant research and fine craftsmanship have produced a consistent elegance of designs. In all domains, Marc Bohan seeks the rare quality that is the symbol, the very essence of beauty. Accessories finish a fashion look and are an inexpensive way to keep up-to-date in fashion.

"Our way of living has changed drastically in the past ten years and will continue to change in the future". Leisure time will be accented. This will be an important factor in designing for the changing needs of people. A new emphasis will be placed on traveling with ease, and clothing to fulfil that desire will be needed. Marc Bohan continues to express and assert his ideas while preserving the Dior image and adapting it to modern conceptions.

Krizia

Krizia is the name of a character in a plato dialogue concerning a woman's vanity. Maricuccia Mandelli, who has taken the name Krizia for her firm, caters to the woman who instinctively knows what is the right choice for her, and each of her Krizia collections offer a woman the freedom to choose from a range of directions.

For the year 2002, Mandelli foresees simplicity, comfort, and functionality in styles (elastic for complete freedom of movement); fabrics (crease-resistant); and accessories (essential) Maricuccia Mandelli also believes that the sarong is the epitome of classic fashion. "It existed four thousand years ago and it will travel with us on our voyage to the future".

Karl Lagerfeld for the House of Chloe

"Deep changes in fashion will come with new developments in fabrics technology". But Karl Lagerfeld believes that major fashion changes will not occur until the year 1990. Lagerfeld, who is working with the company that produces Trevira, is continually offered new materials to work with and appraise. "The body is the most important thing of the future. People today like very active sports. There is new freedom for the woman of the future—a new sense of identity with a much more relaxed attitude". "Couture" refers to dresses that are made to order. In the past, couture created an image, but Lagerfeld feels that there is no longer a need for couture, especially since most women wear smaller sizes. Today and in the future, "women fit the dress; the dress is not fitted to the women". The ebb and flow of fashion's future will continually bring about the different waves; there will be a quality wave, and then a cheap wave; a fun wave, and a jewelry and ornamentation wave. At times there will be quieter moments and also ethnic moments. Fashion will always repeat itself, but there will always be continues change.

Jean-Claude De Luca

"The future belongs to women ....." the women of the year 2002 will be a conqueror—sure of herself, self-confident, likable, a woman of many facets. She has passed the stage of emancipation and thus no longer needs to be aggressive. She will not be a sweet a woman, nor she will be a woman object. She will be full of vitality, a career woman, aware that working brings her freedom." Very open-minded, she will know that the would belongs to her. She has only to choose. The man in her life, the sex of her children, her body, shape, her culture, her behaviour—good buddy or a romantic, depending upon her mood and her desires. She will be very narcissistic, she will always wish to please, above all, herself.

"There will be new products that will allow her to change the colour of her hair and eyes as she pleases; she will be able to match them to her clothes every day if she so chooses. She will have a basic wardrobe-like-men but no masculine clothing. Three important points for clothing ; function, comfort, and poetry. At the same time clothing will be active, protective and seductive.

Givenchy

"Beauty is elegance," according to Givenchy. His enthusiasm for creation has made his artistic life successful. Givenchy's designs are classic, never less than perfect. Simplicity, balance and unity of design never contradict the fluidity of the fabric.

Kansai Yamamoto

Kansai Yamamoto is confident that soon women will attain complete equality with men. Human beings will have more respect and feeling for one another, and they will see one another as part of a whole. In the past, women instinctively dressed to please men. According to Kansai this attitude will practically disappear. Clothes will not be as draped as they have been, nor will they have many pleats, and ruffles will become extinct. He feels that a woman can look very sensual in mens attire. "People do not have to show off their sex through the clothing that they wear." A similarity in dress between the sexes will result, but individuality will prevail. Life will have been simplified. Kansai believes, and people will indulge in a greater variety of sports and related activities. With this type of life-style, fabrics will be created to absorb body perspiration successfully and enable the wearer to feel comfortable, whether he or she is exercising or strolling. For evening, the future will bring a greater for dancing. This form of entertainment will provide additional exercise, and fashions to highlight the activity will be designed.

At the present time, Kansai has three different lines of clothing; one for the international market, one for the Japanese market, and Kansai 2000—an intensely dramatic fashion concept with a strong military air.

History of Costumes

14 CHAPTER

History of Indian Garments from Ancient to Modern Times

Indian culture dates far back in history. Its beginning stems from the golden age of a civilization unearthed at '**Harrappa and Mohenjodaro**' in Sind. The excavations from these buried towns show that people who dwelt in the Indus valley more than 4000 years ago, wore a robe with or without embroidery over the left shoulder and under the right arm, extending well below the knees, and another skirt like garment which was secured round the waist by a cord which might have been either a form or breeches or alternatively a close clinging dhoti. The women were bare to the waist, except for the jewelry and were draped below in scanty skirts which ended above the knees. The skirt was held by a girdle made of strings or beads or bands of woven material secured by a broach or fastening of some kind. Sometimes in the cold weather cloak was wrapped round the upper part of the body, but it did not extend below the hem of the skirt, it only covered the arms without concealing the breasts.

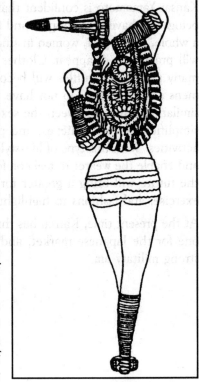

Women sometimes wore a fan-shaped head-dress, but no footwear was worn by either sex. Both men and women kept long hair parted in the middle and coiled in a ring on top of the head, or in similar rings concealing the ears. Sometimes the hair was gathered up in a knot or bun and secured by a fillet which circled the forehead. Combs and hair pins were sometimes worn in the hair and thin ribbons of gold with decorative pendants were used as ornaments on the sides of the head. Ornaments like pendants, **earrings**, coils of gold or

silver, necklaces with rows of beads with different shapes,
bangles, anklets and finger rings of various shapes, bangles,
anklets and finger rings of various shapes were in use. There is
evidence to show that the ladies of 'Mohenjodaro' were adept
in the use of make-up and used khol and lipsticks to beautify
themselves.

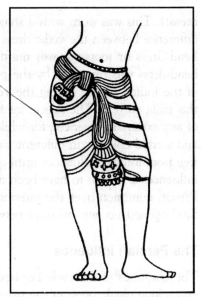

The Aryans were inhabitant of northern India i.e., Punjab and
Kashmir. The Aryan conquest swept over the 'Sumerians' down
to the south were the refugees settled down to become the
ancestors of the 'Dravedians'. In their acclimatization to the
warmer environments of their new home, the Dravedians gave
up their winter cloaks, long hair and beards but retained their
original apparel and ornaments.

The prevalent fashion of the rolled and bifurcated loin clothes
worn by both sexes in South India answered the description of
the men's clinging dhotis and the scanty skirts of the women.
The Nair women of the south are used to being bare to the
waist while a few of the medieval, feminine south Indian fashions
of hair styles are very similar to those discovered in the
'Mohenjodaro' excavations.

Vedic Age

The principle article of the Indian dress in the vedic age was a
long piece of cloth plain or dyed, often with fringes and borders.
This was girded round the loins and tied at the waist either in
front or on the sides with artistic knots, elaborate frills and
crinkles displaying the gorgeous border. The border formed a
distinctive part of the fabric. The waist cloth was sometimes
put on in the form of a divided skirt a vogue confined to the
men. The other end of the cloth which was not displayed had
a shorter and plainer border. The word 'Nivi' was used, to
describe the women's lower garment and ancient writings have
referred specifically to the ornamental tasseled border and to
the knot which held the garment in place. The blossom and
shoulders were covered by another separate garment which
was either a loose wrap consisting of an ample scarf of light
texture. This scarf was drawn across on cross-wise over the
bust and tied at the back, to serve as bodice or was even a
short and tight tailor-made jacket, e.g., 'KANCHOLIKA',
KURPASEKA', and 'STANDANSUKA' (a covering for the

breast). This was worn with a shawl or an additional "Raimant" covering it. The difference between the vedic dress of men and women was very insignificant. No head-dress or footwear was maintained except during rituals. The use of the head-dress was restricted by the prevalent fashions of hair-dressing the clothing of the Indian people during the vedic and epic ages was not very different from this main pattern. The reason for its endurance was the almost complete absence of any external influences, for while the earlier vedic Aryans themselves migrated and started colonies in different parts of the world their own land was practically free from foreign influences until about the Buddhist times. The earliest of these influences is known to have been made by the "Persian" in the year 516 B.C. The Persian dominion over the province of North-Western Punjab and the whole of Sind opened up new avenues between the Persian and Indian civilization.

The Persian Influence

The costumes of the early Persians consisted of loose trousers and a long cloak, open in the front. The costumes used by the 'KUSHAN' kings of India... i.e., consisted of a pointed cap, a tunic, an open coat, trousers and heavy high boots. Another common form of 'mkushan' coat was fastened at the side, very similar to the Mughal "Jalan". The attire might have been the archetype of the long coat, the loose straight trousers, now worn by people in Sind and parts of Punjab, though the trousers are often reminiscent, more of the Chinese, than of the Persian style. It is significant that a similar garment also forms part of the national dress of the Pareses of Bombay and Sind who migrated from their homeland to India.

The Greek Influence

Two hundred years after the Persian invasion India was raided by the forces of 'Alexander the Great' in the course of the years many Indo-Greek dynasties gradually rose to power along the North-West frontiers of India and ruled over Punjab for more than a hundred years. As a result, the influence of the Greek culture spread over the North-Western parts of India down to 'Kathiawar'. One of the consequences of the Greek conquest of Asian territory was the gradual Helenisation of the lands they conquered. While the Greeks in India tended to become rapidly Indianised in their religious and ceremonial beliefs. They did not fail to Helenise Indian sculpture and many of the other useful arts and crafts in India. Greeks, like all people born in mild climate were used to significant nakedness and their usual costume bared a great part of their body. Their normal dress consisted of two garments each of which was nothing more elaborate than an oblong piece of woolen cloth. The undergarment or tunic 'Chiton' was folded round the body, pinned over each shoulder and its hanging folds caught and held in place by a girdle at the waist. The men's tunic fell to the knees and the women's a little lower. Over the tunic was thrown a cloak of somewhat thicker material, which in winter could be wrapped tightly round the body on in summer so arranged so as to leave the limbs more free. This cloak or 'Himatio as it was called was a large form covered piece of cloth which was thrown over the left shoulder and held firmly with the arm then drawn away on the back towards the right side over the under the right arm; and then again over the left shoulder or left arm. The 'Himation'

generally reached to the knee or a little lower. To wear it too long was considered a sign of extravagance or pride. The mild climate often permitted the men to dispense with the 'Himation' and go about in the simple 'Chiton' but the 'Chiton' as a simple article of dress was never used by the women except in the house. Saddles and boots of various types were used, but no hat was worn except on journeys.

In India the apparel which closely resembles the tunic is the 'Phiren' of the Kashmir. The 'Phiren' is a long woolen shirt hanging down to the ankles when worn by the women but not so low in the case of the men. It has loose sleeves and an open collar. It is slipped down the neck and with its heavy folds and cultural waist band, it is very similar to the 'doric' tunic after making allowances for variations due to time, fashion and locality. The origin of this costume has been traced to the time of king 'Harshada' (about 11th century A.D.) but probably it is much older. This with the Greek settlement in India, the use of 'shawls' and 'Mantles' (Chadars) was introduced as the Greeks were accustomed to a similar wrapping garment or cloak.

There is a striking resemblance between the dress of the central Asian 'Uzbek' girls and the 'Kashmir' girls gown. As in Kashmir the 'Kirghiz' the feminine head-dress is fitted with long ear flaps to which are attached long coral or silver ornaments. There is the same open necked loose sleeved gown, the same long cape reaching to the waist band, all indicating a common Greek origin, but the most obvious Greek influence is noticeable in the 'Draperies'. The impression of extension and fluidity given by the skirted part of the robes and the presence of longer vertical folds shown in the outer surface can be seen in the ancient sculptures.

These vertical folds seem to have been projected by stretching apart the lower garment upward to form a drapery for the dress and shoulder or alternatively by allowing the upper garment to be long enough to serve as a covering for the lower limbs. It was this classical trait which became the model of the 'Saree' as it came to be worn in later times allover India after the real differences leveled up by a gradual process of fashion integration and confluence in the country.

Helenism continued to be the influencing force in India. This was the time when a Buddhist culture was also flourishing in a country with its ideals of monastic life and renunciation. Buddhism tended to restrain the extravagance and sensuousness of human needs and possessions. It vigorously tried to suppress the Helenic influence by simplification of dress in the regions where the Greek spirit had not yet penetrated. A characteristic feature of sculptures of Northern India of this period is the falling skirt of which the ends drop loosely down to the ankles instead of passing between the legs and being tucked at the back.

In Bengal and Uttar Pradesh the cloth tied round the waist among the male population is distinguished by an interfemoral tuck of the plain end at the back. The style originated in the south, as in Madhya Pradesh and most parts of South India the fashion is common in both sexes. The monotony of the light posterior tuck left no display of borders encouraged by Northern fashion. The wearing of the 'kunch' or the posterior tuck is not special Hindu custom.

The Hindu women of Gujarat are not used to it but Maharashtrian women are. The reason is that while Gujarat has mainly been a land of peace, Maharashtra has been the scene of many wars, where women might be raped or abducted and where the 'kunch' might give them a slightly additional protection and a chance to escape. It is much easier to run with 'kunch'.

Indian history saw the settlement of the Persians, the Greeks and the Kushans in the country. The racial stamp of these foreign conquerors was marked upon the inhabitants of Western Punjab and they are believed to have given birth to turn of the noblest tribes known in Indian history as the 'Jats' and the 'Rajputs'. The Rajput dynasty came into power in about the middle of the seventh century and continued to rule over India till the end of the twelfth century. Little is known about the social and domestic life of the people, ruled by the Rajputs during those five hundred years. The sculptors depict scantiness of attire and superfluous jewelry. The loin cloth assumed a sharper shape and couture and had a definite tucked portion. The tunic was based on the monastic robes. The female attire was in two pieces. The forms of which suggested, the making of a skirt a light scarf and a short breast-pan was also beginning to gain favour among the stylish woman of this period. The skirt was made of Muslin, intended to be wrapped around the lower limbs and in some cases held around the waist by a belt. It reached down to the feet. In South-India this was the sole attire of the women. In Kashmir the garment consisted of a woollen robe covering the arms and breast, fitting without a wrinkle and falling too the heels from the upper part of the hips. In winter the face was covered with a mantle but ordinarily covered with a nose veil. The head was adorned with a pale red turban. In other parts the upper portion of the body was tightly laced into a little jacket and covered by means of a light tunic or kerchief.

The Purdah System

Between the years 1000 and 1500 A.D. India passed through one of her most fitful periods in history. Throughout this period the whole of Punjab and its eastern fringes continued to be the field of increasing battles during which the throne of 'Delhi' was tossed amongst a number of Afghan rules. The predatory activities of many of these vandal chieftains who practiced slavery and restricted the freedom of Indian women. Between the captors who kept her jealously guarded, and the parents who kept her closely sheltered, the woman found herself enveloped in a veil, the folds of which became impenetrable with the passage of time.

The chivalrous Rajput to whom the honor of his family was dearer to him than his life and who was a member of the ruling order was exposed to the worth and vengeance of the invaders, was compelled more than anyone else to protect his woman from the conquerors. The Rajput ladies were conscious about their chastity, and were quick in realizing the danger of appearing unveiled in public.

The prevailing dresses of the Indian woman were decollete and similar clothing which was apt to reveal the charms of the fair sex. The peril she faced in the disturbed condition of the country made it necessary to cover herself more besides remaining hidden, behind doors. This was revolutionary for the Indian people and their dress as they had never in the past been determined by prudish ideals.

The first step towards the increase of dress had been taken when the primitive single body garment had been split up into two separate pieces. These pieces were (ondhni), which was expected to veil the body more effectively than the slack wrapping of the sarees. The next step was to replace the unstitched wrapping of the waist cloth by a skirt. The art of stitching was not unknown to the Indians, and the transition was achieved quickly.

The Rajputs being the principle opposers of the Muslim, accomplished the reforms in their own interest. A tailored costume was welcome for the sake of the variations in shape, cut and design which it permitted. The bodice of the fifteenth century period was a smart and light jacket rigidly bound by means of tapes and ribbons. These ribbons were fastened in front. Another article of dress named 'Kurti' which was a short shirt like female dress falling from the shoulders to the middle of the body with sleeves and lapels which had sashes both on the right and left sides. Such a garment offered a covering for the upper part of the body from the throat to the navel.

The fifteen century cholis of 'Gujarat' also clothed the trunk upto the waist. The covering of the thorax was made of two garments. The short inner bodies of a highly decorative material unconcealed by the outer blouse, might have possibly been a diminutive apron attached to the lower edge of the bodice. A fashion which is observed even today by some gypsy tribe of Central India.

There is no evidence to show that the sleeves of these bodice as worn in Northern India covered the entire arms upto the wrist. Since that curtailed the use of jewelry of which the ladies were exceptionally fond of. But the entire object of making the Rajput woman inconspicuous was not successful as guided by the hand of nature, she was able by means of artful touches to convert what was to her a curtain on her beauty, into something which gave it a favourable setting.

The prevalence of these Rajput dresses was a limited trend. West of Jamuna, including Rajasthan, the people of the South and the East disfavoured this tendency towards over clothing due to their climate and moreover they were free from the apprehensions which induced the people in the north to make such experiments. The Indian costume did not undergo much change during this period. The dhoti had come to stay as the sole national male costume of the country. Although in the domain of the Rajputs the aristocracy sometimes favoured the long coats and turbans and those who like more clothing wore trousers lined with so much cotton that would surface for a number of counter-panes on saddle lugs. These trousers had no visible openings and they were so huge that they covered one's fatness. The strings by which they were

Ancient

fastened were at the back. The 'Sidan' a piece of dress covering the head and the upper part of the breast and neck, was also fastened at the back with buttons. The Kashmir male still wore the woollen shirt over which he now put on the girdle. The use of the turban was prohibited to him under the, Muslim religion, but he wore the 'Chakma' and 'Dulak' on his feet. He called his woolen shirt 'Phirren' which was a variation of the Persian word 'Pairhan' or shirt. In the Deccan the men wore more jewellery and very little clothing. In Gujarat men wore 'Dhotis' reaching down to the ankles, with a short scarf thrown across the shoulders leaving the upper part of the body uncovered. A kind of peaked cap or 'Mukut' was usually used as a head-dress. The feet were usually bare but wooden clogs were used sometimes. Footwear with a long, painted forepart believed to be relics of the reign of the 'Khilji' and 'Lodhi' kings of Delhi. On gala occasions of waist band of shy cloth was tastefully fastened over the *dhoti*. The essentials of the male costume have remained unaltered.

Ancient

Modern

The History

15 CHAPTER

Origin of the Royal Attire (Salwar-Kameez)

Individuality, adaptability and faith in coexistence are the attributes of Indian costumes. Inspite of the plurality of patterns, inspite of strong local and regional identity, a certain fundamental unity runs through all the vast and varied array of our dresses. This unity in diversity due to a common bond of a common heritage, is as much as character of our sartorial culture as of our style of living.

This is the expression of our culture and the story of the *Salwar-Kameez* in all its splendid finery. From its humble beginning, the *Salwar-Kameez* still retains its original fluidity. This is an account of how the *Salwar-Kameez* has evolved down the ages from the begining of the Persian era to the present age.

Aesthetically dress serves two purposes—it helps to enhance the beauty of the human form and conceals what is not shapely or beautiful by intelligently designing artificial folds, lines and curves on the clothes.

Historical events have been of great significance in changing the style of our dresses. The invasion of Alexander introduced the Hellenic touch. The Muslim influence gifted us the *Sherwani* and *Chudidhar*, *Pyjamas*, the *Kameez* and *Salwar*. Man's thinking changes, so do the dresses. On one hand it is an imitation of the old, on the other an adjustment to the new needs, tastes and circumstances. Interestingly, many coins of the Gupta dynasty in the 4th and 6th centuries, show the emperors wearing tight fitting half sleeved tunic and tight fitting trousers of the *Chudidhar* type. Between 1000 and 1500 A.D. the throne of Delhi was tossed from one dynasty to another and in the disturbed conditions it became necessary to protect women. The conquerors wore tight fitting trousers and a tight sleeved long coat which flared into a full skirt.

The dresses of their women were like that of Persian princesses. In the earlier centuries women were accustomed to the use of a gathered shoulder scarf. If then began being used as a real covering for the breast, back, shoulders and head. It was called *Orhni* which literally meant a covering. At a very late stage of modification was adopted by stitching the two vertical ends of the lower garment. It became like a *ghagra* or *lehenga*.

After the Mughal emperor, Akbar, had ruled for four decades, there appeared a change in the dressing style. The main elements of the costume were the coat, the turban and the trousers. Over a full sleeved garment was worn the half sleeved long coat. The coat was fitted tightly at the waist and then like a skirt reached below the knees.

Wives of the noblemen and officials and high ranking ladies bewitched with the magnetic influence and beauty of the Mughal style, adopted the Mughal *Jama (Kameez)* with flowing skirt, the tight trousers and the *orhni*. The diaphanous *Jama* went out of fashion in 1610 and was not considered fit for the public wear. It was then worn only by entertainers.

Aurangzeb continued to dress magnificently like his royal ancestors. During his reign the skirt of the *Jama* was widened and lengthened. The 18th century saw the story of a disintegrated mughal empire moving steadily towards its final collapse and the rise of the British power. Even the constumes of Shivaji copied the Mughal style in its main features.

The *Jama* was increased its outlandish proportion with waistline rising upto the chest and the long skirt brushing the ground. The trousers became baggy. As the century advanced, the trousers were made close fitting so as to give a feel of the muscular power of the limbs. In places far away from the Rajput and Muslim courts, the difference between Hindu and Muslim costumes were reduced to the minimum. In Kashmir, women of both communities dressed alike. In Punjab, the women, whether Hindu or Muslim, had a common style of trousers or skirt, accompanied by a full sleeved long shirt. In Bengal both the communities dresses in the same manner.

In the last quarter of the eighteenth century, three types of female costumes indicate the Muslim influence, the Rajput influence and the future trends. In the first type a long frock like garment was worn with an opening in the front held by two clasps. A shirt was worn under this and a veil accompanied it. The second type comprised a skirt, a bodice and a diaphanous veil. In the third type the lady wore the second type, but with a longer piece of *orhni* which was used not only to cover the head, but also a part of the back, the right thigh and back. This is of great significance in the history of Indian costumes. The *orhni* with its increased length covered the head, passed over the breast, coming down to find tucking holds at the waist, circled it round the ends in the front, with graceful folds from the navel down to the ankle. The *orhni* being a very thin texture did not totally suppress the presence of the two garments covered by it.

In the declining days of the Mughal empire, men wore heavy coats and the lower garment was a pair of loose but straight *pyjama*. Even Raja Ram Mohan Roy adopted the Muslim dress although he came from an orthodox family.

It must go to the credit of the Indian women that the allure and prestige of the European dress could not tempt them to forsake their sartorial heritage. The *Salwar-Kameez*, the *Ghagra-Choli* and the *Saree* appeared to them more graceful than any foreign garment.

The *Salwar-Kameez* was worn along with a light scarf looped over the shoulders. Even the saree cannot compete with this sartorial ensemble for its multipurpose character, especially in the field of sports. Running, jumping, playing and exercises, requiring vigorous movements, are restricted in a *Saree*. *Salwar* is the only bifurcated lower garment that matches the English trousers in its utility.

Its psychological appeal to the Indian mind rests on the fact that assuring a complete freedom of the movement to the body, the *salwar* maintains the female decorum by keeping the legs covered all the time. Indian woman have generally kept their legs covered from time immemorial. Educational institutions also preferred *Salwar-Kameez* as the school uniform. This dress also came to the aid of teenagers who found themselves too grown up to flaunt a frock and yet not too old to be offered a *saree* by their mothers. The tight fitted *Pyjamas* of the Mughal women was considered too revealing and therefore the fashion dictated a medium width that would blur the outline of the legs and thighs. However, it started growing to varying lengths at different places till it took a loose baggy shape with narrow openings at the legs. Slowly it became the craze of all women and its width went on increasing till it got the shape of the *ghagra*.

A Punjabi Dress

After some years was the trend reversed once again and the *salwar* became less floppy and more body fitting. The *Kameez*-also went through several changes before it could reach its present form. Its length fluctuated. First it dropped down to the knees in 1920's and then rose up to look like an English frock in the 30's and again descended to the knees by the 50's.

Another change in the *Kameez* was brought about by designing it on the lines of the European frock. But not satisfied with this style, a new craze started dressing its girth to make it cling to the body. In the late 60's the lower part of the *Kameez* was so tightly worn around the hip line that the wearer could hardly walk with ease. However, the *Salwar-Kameez* throughout all this gave a coveted delicacy and spring like smartness to the youthful form while giving a look of freshness, slimness and poise.

Though women did not copy the European dress, their liberal attitude helped them to experiment with the regional dress.

Salwar-Kameez and *Orhni* of Punjab

The Punjabi women took to the *Saree* and the girls of Bengal tried to experiment with *Salwar-Kameez*. Thus rigid demarcations between dresses among different communities, classes and religious groups got somehow obliterated through mutual exchange and imitation of various styles.

In Punjab, men wear silk *Kurtha* and *Pyjamas*. *Churidhar* is another version of the trousers. Its fits closely like a glove from the ankle to the knee. It is tailored in a special way by cutting the cloth in a diagonal section (bias) and stitching the pieces in a prescribed arrangement. The upper portion of the garment remained loose. This type of *Churidhar* trousers were worn by Hindu and Muslim women of upper classes during the Mughal period.

An Eleventh Century Attire

The *Churidhar* satorially links up Punjab with Rajasthan. The female dress comprises *Salwar-Kameez* and *Orhni*. The Punjabi *Salwar* is tailored in many styles, sometimes a little baggy and sometimes gathered near the ankles causing vertical folds. A new style was emerged with the upper part of the *Salwar* narrowed to neatly and closely fit the waist and abdomen. Among the modern styles the *Churidhar-Kameez-Orhni* combination is also popular. The *Kameez* is a long knee length tunic with half sleeves or long sleeves tapering to the wrists. Sometimes the skirt of the *Kameez* is flared below the waist.

The scarf variously known as *dupatta, orhni, chunni* or *chunari* was formerly used to cover the head and screen the face from public view. The middle part of this long cloth rests on the head, the right end is looped across the breast and the left shoulder while the left end is allowed to hang freely.

Muslim rulers were the first from outside whose impression on the Indian costume was deeper and wider than what meets the eye. It indirectly influenced the costume of women allover India.

It is also pointed out that a representation of the queen of a Persian king of the 5th century A.D. shows her wearing a trousers, an article of attire worn by the Persian women in present day. The *Dupatta* or Upper Cloth was used for effect. It was capable of fashionable variations. It is a sedate and dignified mode of wear, almost all modes being identical with those affected by males and is the same for a female of the north-

The Attire of the H.P. Women

west as well as Mathura. The use of *dupatta* in the image of the Greco Buddhistic period as a second covering horizontally over the lower back must be attributed to the desire of the wearer for the graceful effect of lateral folds in a dressfull of vertical and oblique folds in the front. It is highly reminiscent of the use of shawl by orthodox females till recently.

Costume is a cultural visual, a mirror of the times and the people. The dress of people presents a vital clue to their mood and taste, their aesthetic temper, their art and skill to adjust to their social and geographical environment and to the way of living.

It was the Mughal costume that first awakened in the minds of the people, a desire for the over-clothing. It developed the feeling to appear graceful. The second impact was more on a psychological plane.

Generation after generation when people saw the perpetual picture of fully draped human forms all round them, they became generally conscious that their own dress did not fully cover their body. New attitudes and values started sprouting. They realised that more dress could only bring them more protection. They wanted to be doubly sure, secure and wrapped. This Psychological process was virtually responsible in shaping new fashions and dresses.

SALWAR-KAMEEZ

The Decades-old Indian Attire (Advent)

Salwar-Kameez has been a part of the Indian attire for decades. Even in the 40's *Salwar* was visible on the Indian horizon. Though women were more prone to be seen in the 'wrapparel' other modes of dresses were also part of the Indian fashion culture.

A Kashmiri Costume

The reason for the popularity of the *Saree* was and is mainly the fact that the country is economically not very sound. The pro rata income has been one of the lowest in the world. The *Saree* was an apparel which could be wrapped around by any female member of the household. Sisters, mothers and daughters could drape the some *Saree* on different occasions. Thus one garment could be used by several members of a family. This was one of the main reasons for the popularity of the *Saree*.

The basic *Saree* comprised of six metres of cloth of different makes. Designs and borders were added to this wrapparel to enhance its appeal. In the north the

Chunari Saree, featured repeatedly in the ancient paintings, made their appearance. Though *Saree* was the main apparel for women, other modes of attire were also taking shape. The *Salwar-Kameez* was also apparent on the Indian scene.

But the *Salwar* was confined to only certain locales, like the *chunari choli* which was restricted to Rajasthan and Kutch, the *Salwar* stayed within the confines and boundaries of Punjab.

Initially the *Salwar* was a loose fitting apparel. It was extremely loose near the ankle and tapered down to a narrow designed paicha. This was also called the *Peshawari Salwar*. These were not only confined to ladies but even the gents doned them.

These however, failed to gain acceptance among the masses, till the 60's when the women became more emancipated. Education, became an essential part of life. This also encouraged women to improve their financial status by seeking employment.

The Indian women, who were now in a better financial position, got these suits tailor-made. Perhaps the first non-Punjabi Indian actress to appear on the screen in *Salwar-Kameez* was Geeta Bali in 'Alamara'.

Movies always played a dominant role in creating fashion conscionusness and it was only in the 70's that our heroines started scampening across the screen draped in body hugging *Salwar-Kameez* suits. These were tight fitting *Salwar* and skin tight *Kameez* with slits on the sides and on the back.

These were later changed. The *Kameezes* were embroidered and patch-work was done to adorn them.

A Sixteenth Century Dress

Movie was the media which set the fashion trend. In fact a successful movie with dazzling dresses often made the fashion statement. But even now, the *Salwar-Kameez* had not gripped the imagination of the masses. Purchasing textiles, going to the tailor and then to the embroider for getting a dress made was a tedious and time consuming procedure. It was, Therefore, not surprising to find the *saree*, still dominating the fashion scene.

It was only in the 80's that *Salwar-Kameez* came into its own. In the late 70's the RMG industry featured into this field. The designer claims it was during the 80's that there was a boom in the *Salwar-Kameez*. The manufacturers experimented with different embroidery work, patch-work zari zardosi beads and other knick-knacks. The dresses were available off-the-shelf and one could walk in, don the dress, see how it suited the individuals personality before purchasing it. This appraisal of the readymade garment is what made the ready-made *Salwar-kameez* takeoff.

However, this was an off-the-shelf experiment, what really started a revolution was creation of boutiques of its kind to start displaying clothes on the rack. Pipe music, dresses on the rack, sales girls dressed in the organisation's attire set the pulse racing as soon as you entered the shop located at world trade centre. It created ripples on the fashion scene, in air-conditioned ambience. One could brouse through the shop, pick up and peruse any dress that one felt interested in. If one needed advise the friendly sales personnel were always available to offer guidance.

The success of "London Fashions" encouraged others to follow suit and soon a spate of boutiques was evidenced.

The boutiques, however catered to the elite. The price factor discouraged a working women to cross the portals of the shop. It was then these shops started dispensing clothes at reasonable prices that their popularity chart showed a sharp incline.

The ready availability at reasonable rates has encouraged the offtake of *Salwar*, in turn encouraging more entrepreneurs to enter the field of *Salwar-Kameez* manufacture.

Today, *Salwar-Kamez* in literally hundreds of styles, has almost become ubiquitous allover the country. With hundreds of boutiques displaying thousands of styles, ladies have a multitude of dresses to select from. However, with the face pace in change in fashions, the designers have to keep on their toes. The highbrow designers normally design garments which cannot imagine a girl flaunting at a party or walking into an office with.

They are normally outlandish which can be worn more for shock effect. But members of the clothing manufacturers association have been generally more down-to-earth and their designs can be donned for any occasion.

Mughal Jama with Flowig Skirt

So, how do you keep pace with the changing tastes of their clientele. They have to keep a finger on the psyche of the individual. The designers, at present, know that the electronic media plays an important role in setting fashion trends. Television has become an important media of communication in influencing fashion trends. The designer confess that they pick up the fashion idea from the oversea's channels being beemed by the satellite, which forms the staple diet of the present day generations as far as entertainment is concerned. Being glued to television, they are psyched into western attire. It was therefore imperative for the Indian designers to come up with creations that would make these youngsters go ga-ga. And we have a *Kameez* designed like a long coat! You want an Indian touch? Have it embroidered.

A new concept has been painting, to give it the designer effect. As no two pieces are painted alike, you have designer *Kameezes* with parallel *Salwars*. The *dupatta* is given to go by to make the *Salwar-Kameez* not only more economical but to display the design on the *Kameez* will continue to rule the roost as far as the Indian fashion scene is concerned for. The Indian women has, from childhood been taught to be attired in a manner which does not encourage nudity. And the *Salwar-Kameez* covers more than even the *Saree*. Besides, it also hides the Indian woman's aptitude for flabby waistline.

No body (designer) can make the woman change her dressing habits. And, most of the designers state, it would not be easy for them to get attuned to the Indian Psyche to design apparel suitable for them.

As far as the *Salwar-Kameez* is concerned it would take them years to design suitable dresses for Indian women. That is why they have stuck to something safe, like casuals, said one of the prominent designers. But one thing that can be assured is that always even in future this attire *Salwar-Kameez* will have a continuing popularity.

Chinese Revolution 16th-21st Century

CHAPTER 16

The Art of Traditional Chinese Dress

A clatter and crash of drums and gongs sound at a theater of Chinese Opera in Taipei as a young warrior appears on stage in traditional Chinese costume. From his head ascend two tall plumes, tracing in the air each movement and gesture he makes. Some might think these plumes are simply ornamental, but in fact they originate in the battle wear of the Warring States period (475-221 B.C.). Two feathers of a ho bird (a kind of pheasant good at fighting) were inserted into the headwear of warriors of this period to symbolize a bold and warlike spirit, like that of the ho. An outstanding characteristic of traditional Chinese clothing is not only an external expression of elegance, but also an internal symbolism. Each and every piece of traditional clothing communicates a vitality of its own. This combination of external form with internal symbolism is clearly exemplified in the pair of fighting pheasant feathers used in headwear.

Objects found in archaeological remains of China's Shantingtung culture, which flourished over 18,000 years ago, such as bone sewing needles, and stone beads and shells with holes bored in them, attest to the existence of the concept of ornamentation and the craft of sewing already in that age. Variety and system in clothing were roughly established by the era of the Yellow Emperor and the Emperors Yao and Shun (about 4,500 years ago). Remains of woven silk and hemp articles and ancient ceramic figures further demonstrate the sophistication and refinement of clothing in the Shang Dynasty (16th to 11th century B.C.). The three main types of traditional Chinese clothing are the *pien-fu*, the *Ch'ang-p'ao*, or long robe, and the *shen-i*. The *pien-fu* is an ancient two-piece ceremonial costume, including a tunic-like top extending to the knees, and a skirt reaching to the ankles; one had to wear a skirt on certain occasions in order to be properly dressed. A pen is a cylindrical ceremonial cap; *pien-fu* later came to refer to the whole suit of ceremonial clothes.

The long robe is one-piece garment extending from the shoulders to the heels that was worn by both men and women.

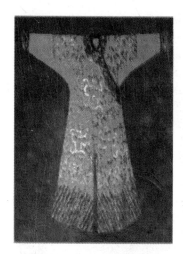

The *shen-i* falls somewhere between the pien-fu and the long robe in its construction. The *shen-i* was made in two sections, tunic and skirt, much like the *pien-fu*; but the two were sewn together, so it is similar to the long robe in appearance. Upon close examination, however, it more closely resembles the *pien-fu* because of its very large cut and deep folds, which draped generously over the body. This is, in fact, the origin of its name, which literally means "deep clothing". The *shen-i* was the most widely worn of the three different types; it was the "Sunday best" of the common people, and moderately formal attire for government officials and scholars, appropriate for both men of letters and warriors.

Typical of these three types of clothing, besides their wide cut and voluminous sleeves, were a design utilizing mainly straight lines, and a loose fit forming natural folds, regardless of whether the garment was allowed to hang straight or was bound with a sash at the waist. All types of traditional Chinese garments, whether tunic and trousers or tunic and skirt, utilized a minimum number of stitches for the amount of cloth used. And because of their relatively plain design and structure, embroidered edgings, decorated bands, draped cloth or silks, embellishment on the shoulders, and sashes were often added as ornamentation. These decorative bands, appliqued borders, and richly varied embroidered designs came to be one of the unique features of traditional Chinese dress. Darker colours were favoured over lighter ones in traditional Chinese clothing, so the main color of ceremonial clothing tended to be dark, accented with elaborate embroidered or woven tapestry designs rendered in bright colours. Light colours were more frequently used by the common people in clothes for everyday and around the house. The Chinese associate certain colours with specific seasons, for example, green represents spring, red is for summer, white for autumn, and black for winter. The Chinese can be said to have a fully developed system of matching, coordinating, and contrasting colours and shades of light and dark in apparel.

Fashion designers today in the Republic of China and Taiwan are finding new ways to freely combine modern fashion aesthetics and trends with traditional Chinese symbols of good fortune. The great wealth of source material has resulted in a plethora of eye-catching designs for children's and young people's clothing, including guardian deities, lions, the eight trigrams, and masks of Chinese opera characters. Another more ancient source of printed, woven, embroidered, and appliqued design for clothes is Chinese bronzes. Some of these distinctive and unusual designs include dragons, phoenixes, clouds, and lightning. Motifs from traditional Chinese painting, whether bold or refined, often find their way into woven or printed fashion designs, creating a beautiful and striking look.

Traditional Chinese macrame has broad applications in fashion; it may be used to ornament borders, shoulders, bodices, pockets, seams, and openings, as well as in belts, hair ornaments, and necklaces. Some successful examples of combinations of modern and traditional fashion elements are the modern bridal tiara, based on a Sung Dynasty design originally worn over a coiled coiffure; the Human Province style embroidered sash made in the traditional Chinese colours of pure red, blue, and green; and traditional sachets and pendants.

In modern Taiwan society, men are frequently seen at social occasions wearing the dignified and refined traditional Chinese long gown. Women often wear the *ch'i-p'ao*, a modified form of a traditional Ch'ing Dynasty fashion, on formal occasions. There are endless variations of height, length, width, and ornamentation in the collar, sleeves, skirt length, and basic cut of this elegant and very feminine oriental fashion. From these examples, it can be seen how traditional Chinese dress is the spring of modern fashion.

In the wax museum of the Chinese Culture and Movie Center in Taipie, and at the Museum of Costume and Adornment of Shih Chien Home Economics College, you can see comprehensive and carefully researched collections of traditional Chinese men's and women's fashions from over the ages. A visit to one of these collections is both enjoyable and educational.

The people of Taiwan not only incorporate traditional Chinese dress into modern life; they have taken the silk making, spinning, and weaving techniques developed by the ancient Chinese a step further, and created modern textile industries around them. Through these industries, ROC residents can enjoy beautiful fashions with traditional features and modern chic.

EVOLUTION AND REVOLUTION

Chinese Dress 1700 to now — 25 June 1997 - July 1998

Through a stunning display of Chinese dress, this exhibition explores the extraordinary changes that have occurred in Chinese society over the last 300 years. The objects range from the sumptuous silk court robes of the Qing Dynasty to the latest designs from young fashion designers from mainland China, Hong Kong and Taiwan.

Select an item of clothing to examine a larger, higher resolution image and learn about its relationship to Chinese social history.

The exhibition looks at change in Chinese culture through the medium of dress and in particular at the impact of social, cultural, political and economic forces on dress design. The focus of the exhibition is urban dress in major centres of population, government industry and trade such as Peking, Shanghai and Canton from the Qing dynasty (1644-1911) to the present day, but with a special emphasis on the last one hundred years. The exhibition thus spans a turbulent period of China's recent history including the fall of the Qing dynasty—the era of the Empress Dowager, the warlord era, civil war, Japanese occupation, Nationalist rule and after the Communist victory, the People's Republic of China and the transition of Hong Kong to Chinese sovereignty on 1 July 1997. It is the profundity of change that has occurred within Chinese society in the course of the past century which motivated the development of this exhibition.

The exhibition draws on the museum's collection of Chinese dress and has been supplemented by loans from the National Gallery of Victoria and from private collections in Australia and Hong Kong.

The exhibition has been conceived chronologically and there are three main sections—court and court related dress of the Qing dynasty, dress from the early 1900's including the evolution of the Cheungsam, post 1949 dress and the ubiquitous 'Mao suit' and the contemporary period featuring fashion by young designers from mainland China, Hong Kong and Taiwan.

In order to realise the exhibition, the museum has worked closely with many individuals and institutions. The post 1949 section of the exhibition has been the result of a close curatorial collaboration with Brisbane based writer and collector Sang Ye. The museum commissioned Sang Ye to assemble a collection of mainland Chinese dress spanning the period 1940's to 1980's. The result is a unique and valuable collection of Chinese dress which documents a fascinating period of recent Chinese history. Where possible Sang Ye conducted oral history interviews with owners, recording the garments significance to the wearer and its relationship to the wider Chinese social, economic and political environment.

To complement the exhibition a special computer interactive has been developed which will allow visitors to explore the meaning of decorative motifs on a selected number of garments that are on display.

Evolution and Revolution: Chinese Dress

1700s-1900s

Through the medium of dress, Evolution & Revolution: Chinese dress 1700's-1990's explores the dramatic cultural, social, economic and political changes which have occurred in mainland China, Hong Kong and Taiwan over three centuries. This history is revealed through the luxurious court robes of the Qing Dynasty (1644-1911); the tight-fitting, side-slitted East-West cheungsam; the ubiquitous Mao suit, symbol of Communist ideology; and the bold new directions of contemporary designers. Written by authors from Australia, mainland China, Hong Kong and Taiwan and rich with visual material, this unique book offers an accessible, informative and inspiring treatment of Chinese history, culture and dress.

FASHION TRENDS

Chinese

Named as the "97 Spring & Summer Shanghai Fashion Trend Information Releasing Comference", this activity will be one of the highlights of the 96 Shanghai International Fashion Culture Festival, showing the present designing level and the fashion trend prediction authority in Shanghai. To bring it into line with the international norms, and to maximize its authority and [Image] leading role, the sponsors of the activity organize this conference on studying the latest trend in the textile and fashion industry world wide and incorporating China's fashion characteristics.

Experts in clothing materials and fashion designing are invited to select 50 groups of woolen, linen, silk, and cotton materials with various thickness, colours and patterns.

The "97 Spring and Summer Shanghai Fashion Trend Information Releasing Conference" highlights four major themes:

— 1. Future Notes

— 2. Metropolis melody

— 3. Weekend Beats

— 4. Cadenza

Fashion Trends and Cultural Influences 1960-present Fashion Trends and Cultural Influences. 1960-present.

Influences on Fashion

Since the 1960s, sources of fashion influence have multiplied. Centers of fashion influence include Paris, Milan, Tokyo, London, New York and Los Angeles. Fashion no longer "trickles down" from couture to the mainstream; fashion directions come from everywhere-various ethnic groups, youth looks from the street, etc. (Gold, 1991).

Silhouettes

1965   The chemise is the important silhouettes of the decade. The chemise's shoulders are natural with an unmarked waist. Hemlines end above the knee. Shoes with low or flat heels are worn with textured and colored pantyhose or tights which coordinate with the outfit.

1969   Variations of the chemise still dominate contemporary silhouettes. Lengths are very short-barely covering the thighs. An A-line silhouette is popular. Corsets and girdles become obsolete. Tights or pantyhose are essential.

1970   Women begin to wear pantsuits on the street; they become a staple in women's wardrobes by the mid-70s. The midi, a mid-calf length skirt, is introduced and rejected.

1975   A soft, natural silhouette with a bloused jacket or sweater and a flared skirt are typical. Skirt lengths have moved gradually downward to just below the knee.

1977   "Dress for Success" a book by John Molloy advises working women to wear feminine versions of the male business suit. The suit was complete with a skirt and bow tie on the blouse. Wearing pants in business situations was advised against, as a result pantsuits loose favour among many.

1981   Moving to a wider shouldered silhouette; shoulder pads are added to everything, Skirt lengths move gradually shorter. The preppy look and the punk look predominate the youth market.

1987   The mini is introduced and bombs. Women's suits become more diverse in styling less uniform-like.

1988   Karl Lagerfeld offers an updated version of the Chanel suit. Glamour is big.

1990   Long over short silhouettes predominate; long shirts or sweaters over leggings, long jackets over short skirts.

1990's   Anything goes: long or short skirts, pants, sweats. Typi cally found is a more natural silhouette/shoulder after the wide, boxy looks of the early 80's. Strong influence from the youth market in casual wear. Casual Fridays at the office.

Ethnic Influences

By the late 1960s, interest in the world's cultures was evident in fashion. Designers stopped "looking to the future for inspiration and began to plunder the world's ethnic minorities. Every culture had something to offer". Fashion designers have since incorporated more and more design elements from other cultures into their lines Contributing to this trend is the fact that ethnic diversity has become more evident in the US. A few examples of ethnic influences found during this time period include:

1963   Hawaiian Influence - "Blue Hawaii" - Elvis film - set in Hawaii.

1965   Russian Influences - "Dr. Zhivago" - Film - set during Russian revolution overcoats worn by Russian military and by Julie Christie, the female lead, in the film inspired coat designs.

1966-68 Indian Influences - Nehru Suit, Beatles.

1972   Chinese Influences - President Nixon visits China; US designers inspired.

1980's   Japanese Influences - Issey Miyake, Hanae Mori, Rei Kawakubo, Kenzo, and Yohji Yamamoto - all were integral in the emergence of Japanese designer as a major force in fashion during the 1980s (Tortora & Eubank, 1994).

1976   Russian Influences - Yves St. Laurent was inspired by Russian influences for his Winter 1976-77 line. In this collection, St. Laurent was inspired elements of European peasant dress   (embroidered folk blouses, milkmaid's tunics, and Cossack [Russian] costume) and transformed them into fabulous couture garments {Craik, 1994}.

1977   Egyptian Influences - King Tut's treasures visit US; US designers inspired; jewellery, makeup and a few clothing items inspired by Egypt (Tortora & Eubank, 1994.) Steve Martin performs "King Tut" on Saturday Night Live. To hear the song.

1984   Western Influence on Chinese Dress - An exhibition of Yves St. Laurent's work is staged in Beijing. A year later the streets of Beijing are full of YSL knock-offs. The Chinese who   saw the exhibit were inspired by his work, in spite of the fact that they had never been exposed to European fashion.

1996   Chinese Influences - Hong Kong returns to Chinese rule; Chinese motifs and silhouettes are strong influence on designers. Many designers incorporate Chinese elements in their lines 1996-97.

Important Designers

Armani - brought soft Italian tailoring to women's wear in the 80's "It is impossible to overestimate the influence of Georgio Armani on late twentieth century fashion. His unstructured, beautifully made suits are high on the wish-lists of all sorts of women". Courreges - Associated with "space age" designs.

Rudi Gernreich - Known for sport clothes and for such radical looks as a topless swimsuit, see-through blouses and 'no-bra' bras in the 1960's. Halston - the quintessential 70's look, soft layered effects, pantsuits or jumpsuits.

Donna Karan - dresses women like herself. Casual, soft looks; lots of knits. Calvin Klein - Klein's signature is immediately recognizable. He has a spare, lean and simple look that makes everything sexy and sophisticated in the subtlest of ways. Or in Klein's own words: "My personal philosophy of style is simplicity. Minimalism to me is the sexiest quality a man or woman can posses." He works in every fashion category for men and women, including tailored clothing, home furnishings and accessories. He has made his name not only through designs that lead, rather than follow the pack, but through a knack for promotion and especially his provocative advertising campaigns, that tick some people off and titillate others, but in every case, make you remember his name (Calvin Klein Profile, 2000).

Karl Lagerfeld - took over Chanel line in 1982.

Ralph Lauren - known for western looks, outdoor wear and use of natural fibre fabrics.

Mary Quant - Influential in the Mod styles of the 1960's. Important for the mini-skirt of the late 1960s. Helped make London a fashion center in the 1960's.

Yves St. Laurent - originated many innovative styles, soft fluid looks, impeccable couture styling, often uses ethnic inspirations. Was as Dior before opening his own house in 1960. YSL "is the designer who most exactly defines the main thrust of fashion" in the early 80's.

SECTION II
Design

Prints

17 CHAPTER

Prints are the impressions of any creative design made over the fabric or garments using paints or dyes during manufacturing process or at any finished stage. Printing signifies the application of colour to the finished fabric to produce the desired patterns which may be floral of (natural) to hide some manufacturing defects.

There are different types of prints such as:

— Classical print
— Floral print
— Stripes print
— Checks print
— Dot print
— Geometrical print
— Directional print
— Self print
— Computerized print
— Mosaic Marble print
— Wild Print
— Animal print
— Abstract print
— Numerical print
— Alphabetical print
— Children's print
— Photo print

1. Classical Print

This is also known as ethnic or traditional print. In this print, classical motifs or traditional art work or traditional collections are used such as mango, elephant with the chariots, old musical instruments etc. The culture of any particular place can also be considered such as tie and dye, batik, block of Rajasthan etc.

Classical or Traditional Print

2. Floral Print

It has the print of varieties of flowers either in bunch or single spotted, huge or small, combination of leaves and other addings.

Here colour combination is very important.

Floral Print

Pin Stripes

3. Stripes

One would have been different types on the garment but would not have noticed it's classifications. We have many types of stripes for instance:

— Pin stripes

— Zigzag stripes

— Spiral stripes

— Zebra stripes

— Diagonal stripes

— Horizontal stripes

— Vertical stripes

— Curved stripes

— Toothpaste stripes

— Lamp post stripes

a. Pin Stripes: These are stripes which is printed lines at hairy distance and mostly two to three colours are used including the background.

b. Zigzag Stripes: It can come in horizontal or vertical but in the shape of zigzag.

Zigzag Stripes

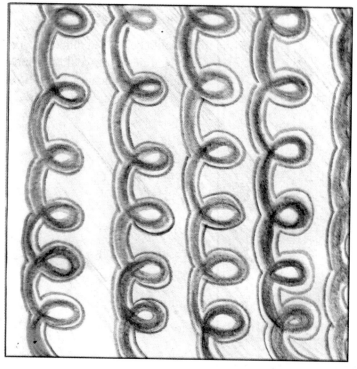

c. Spiral Stripes: This print looks like a stretched spring at medium pressure. this can either be vertical or horizontal.

e. Curved Stripes: This print has the effect of a wave followed either vertical/horizontal.

Spiral Stripes

f. Toothpaste Stripes: This stripe can be multicolored and the distance can vary, but the width of each stripe should be ranging from 0.5-1.5 cms the width of the toothpaste.

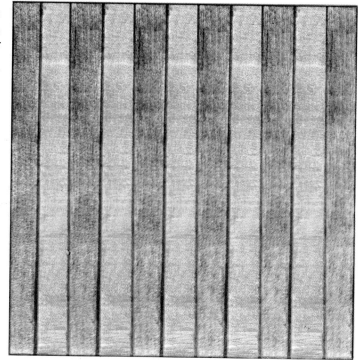

Toothpaste Stripes

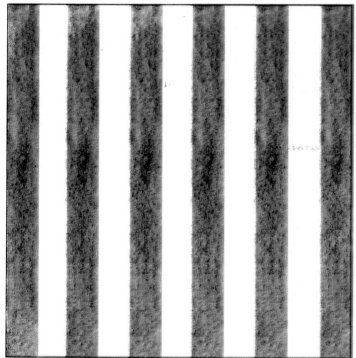

d. Zebra Stripes: In this stripe only two colors are used and mostly neutral coloured scheme is seen. These stripes are placed at equidistance. It is no where related with the texture of a zebra skin. The width of each stripe will not be more than 1.0 cms.

Zebra Stripes

g. Lamp Post Stripes: The width of this print starts from 3-5 cms and it can be a compound stripes too.

All the above said stripes can be printed vertically to be called as vertical stripes, horizontally which is called Horizontal stripes and diagonally for diagonal stripes.

These horizontal, vertical and diagonal has their own characteristic as vertical striped outfit tends to increase the height of the wearer whereas horizontal striped outfit may shorten the look of a person and look more wider.

Lamp Post Stripes

Check Prints

Checks are the prints which is got by intersecting horizontal and vertical lines at ninety degree angles. There are basically four types of checks such as plaids, Madras check, Bombay check and Oxford check.

Plaids are the simple check where all the squares are of equal size and it has the combination of any two colours which are mostly used for the school uniforms. It looks similar to the checks of chessboard.

Plaids (Diagonal)

Madras Check: It has got not more than 2 to 3 vertical stripes with equal (single) horizontal stripes. Typical colours used in Madras Check are blue, red, orange, yellow and white. Now available in all colours. These prints can be used for lungis, shirts, Burmudas and coats.

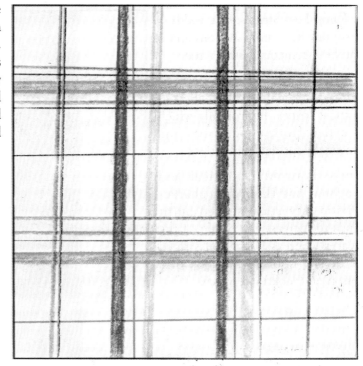

Madras Check

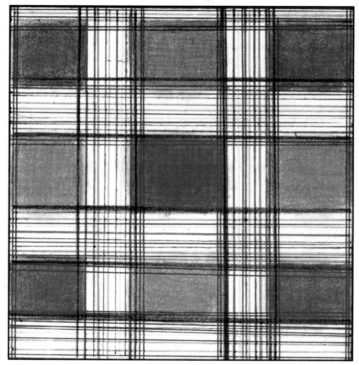

Bombay Check: These checks are mostly available in light colours. Here no proper number of stripes can be counted either horizontally or vertically but stripes are very closely printed.

It is used for shirt materials only.

Bombay Check

Oxford Check: This is found in dark colours with white combination. Here the stripes printed horizontally will be equal to the stripes printed vertically and at equal thickness placed at equidistance. This type of checked fabrics are used for uniforms (school), table mat, bed covers, draperies etc.

Oxford Check

Dots: The dots are the spots either designed or plain and comes in all colours of choice. The dots are basically divided into three types as big dots, small dots and polka dots.

Big Dots are dots which has the radius of 3-10 cms. Some are plain and mostly printed.

Big Dots

Small Dots are dots which are horizontally placed. It can vary from pin dot to radius of 1.5 cms.

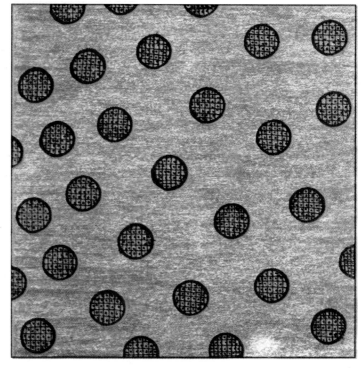

Small Dots

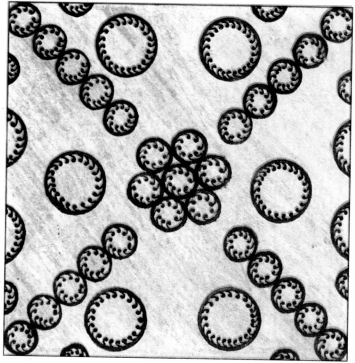

Polka Dots

Polka Dots is a mixture of big and small dots together, usually round or oval shaped with designed filling.

Geometric Print

This is the print where all the geometrical instrument designs are created and the mathematical signs are used such as plus, minus, multiplication, division etc. There is no prescribed color combination.

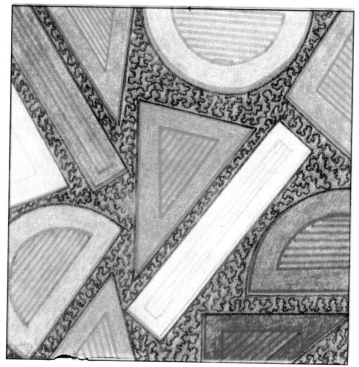

Geometric Print

Directional Prints

Any print which is designed directionally either horizontal, vertical or diagonal is called the directional print. Its feature is to follow the direction of the first one.

This type of print is used in Egyptian dresses.

Directional Prints

Self Prints

Any design which has to be printed should be of the same shades of the background color.

Example: Rubber print.

Self Print

Computerised Print

The designs of this print is taken from computer graphic designs and videogames. Can be used for children and teenagers.

Computerised Print

Wild Print

The effect of the forest with or without animal, nature are used in this print. Mostly dull colours are used.

Example: Camouflage fabric which is used in the uniform of the military men at war.

Wild Print

Animal Print

In a wild print, the nature such as forest with the pictures of animals are used but in Animal print, no wild effect is shown but the importance is given only to the skin texture of the animals and their foot prints such as Zebra, cheetah, Tiger, deer, snake, crocodile, tortoise skin etc.

Animal Print

Abstract Print

This print is made using the irregular shapes with matching colour scheme.

Abstract Print

Numerical Print

Here the numbers from 0-9 are used. Some times with or without mathematical signs.

Numerical Print

Alphabetical Print

Same as Numerical print this print is made using alphabets, wording etc. but cartoons are mostly not used as combination with this.

Example: Newspaper print.

Alphabetical Print

Children's Print

This print consists of designs which can emphasize the children's mood such as cartoon characters, chocolates, fruits, ice creams, toys etc.

Photoprint

The photos of the famous stars, pop singers, old cars etc. are printed on T-shirts which are called photoprint.

Children's Print

Marble Print

This print looks like a marble finish. This can be made by hand in manual process also. For this we require a wide opened pan of water, oil paints/enamels and paper.

Method: Add two to three colours of paint in a pan of water and stir well. It will not get mixed because the oil paints are insoluble in water, they will float. Pass the paper through the water, see that the paint touches the surface of the paper. Dry and preserve.

Photoprint

Necklines

18
CHAPTER

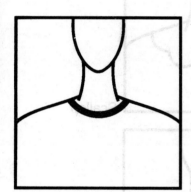

Jewel Neck

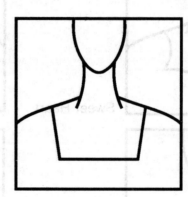

Bucket Neck

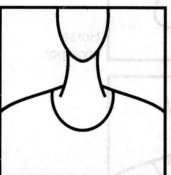

Round Neck

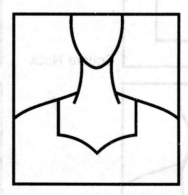

Pentagon

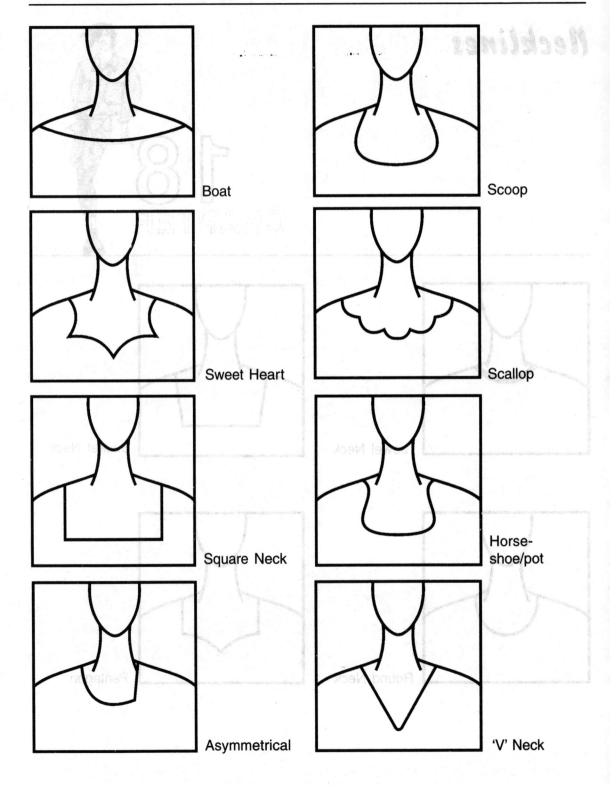

Boat

Scoop

Sweet Heart

Scallop

Square Neck

Horse-shoe/pot

Asymmetrical

'V' Neck

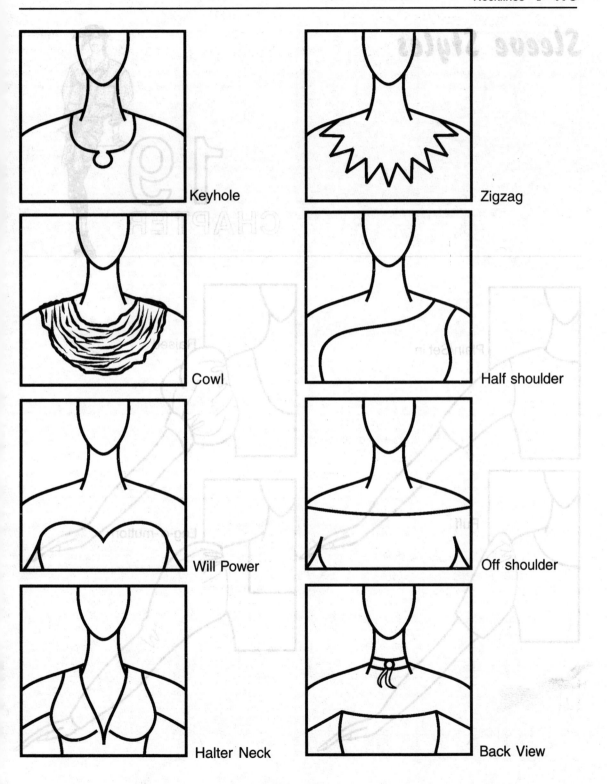

Keyhole

Zigzag

Cowl

Half shoulder

Will Power

Off shoulder

Halter Neck

Back View

Sleeve Styles

19
CHAPTER

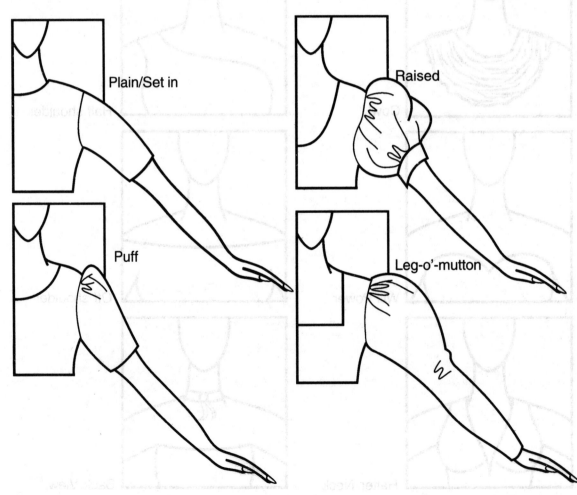

Plain/Set in

Raised

Puff

Leg-o'-mutton

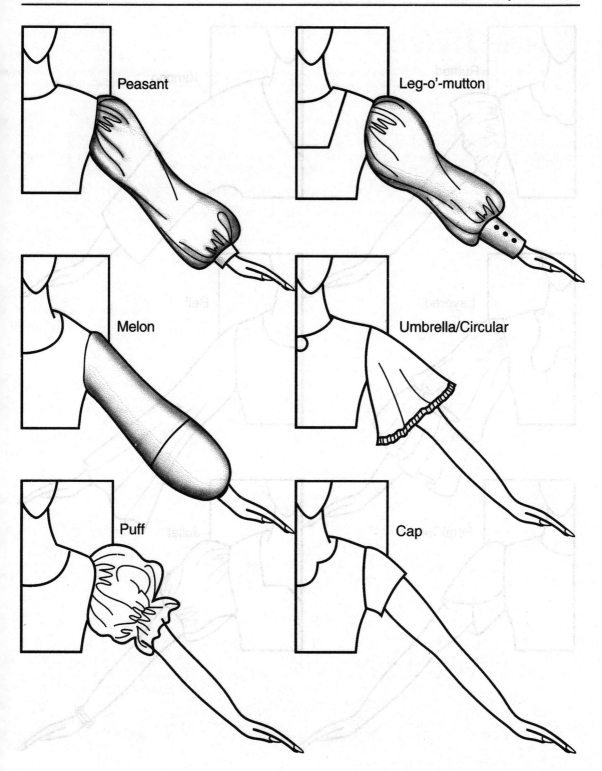

Peasant

Leg-o'-mutton

Melon

Umbrella/Circular

Puff

Cap

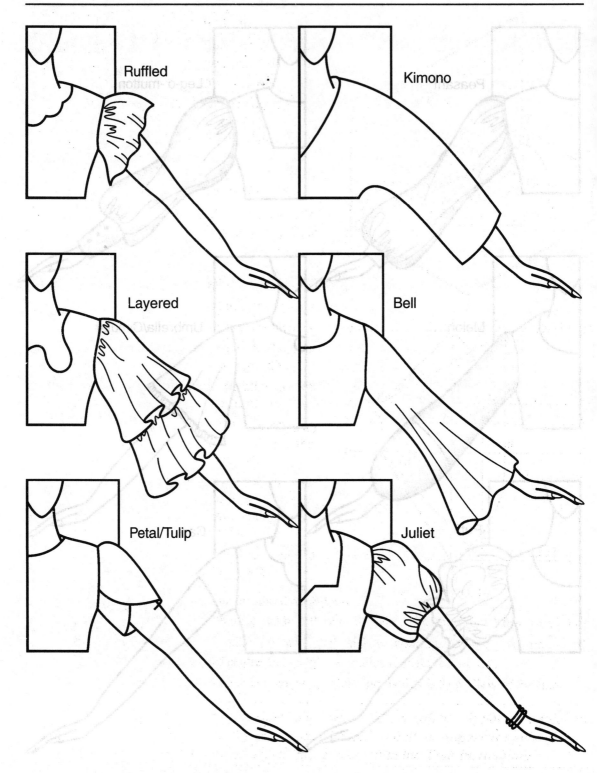

Ruffled

Kimono

Layered

Bell

Petal/Tulip

Juliet

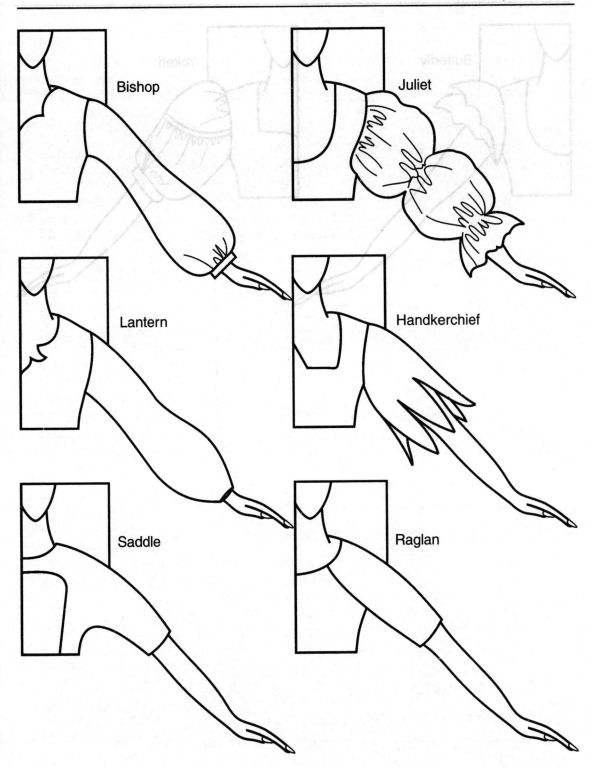

Bishop

Juliet

Lantern

Handkerchief

Saddle

Raglan

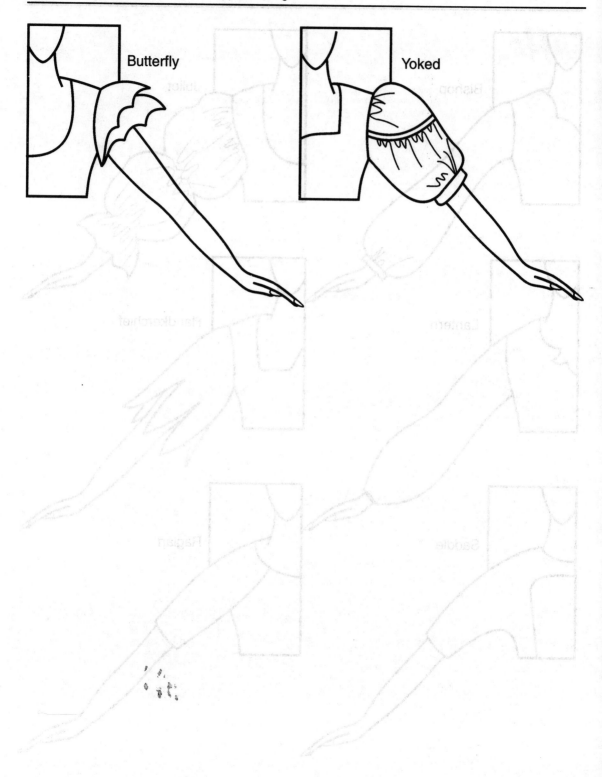

Butterfly

Yoked

Cuffs

20
CHAPTER

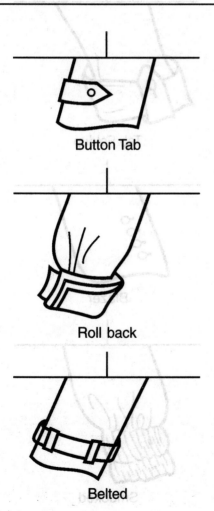

Button Tab

Roll back

Belted

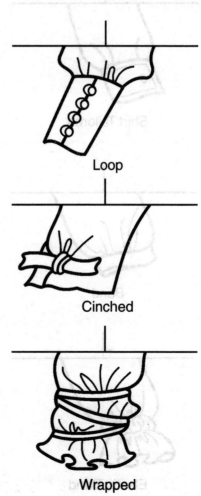

Loop

Cinched

Wrapped

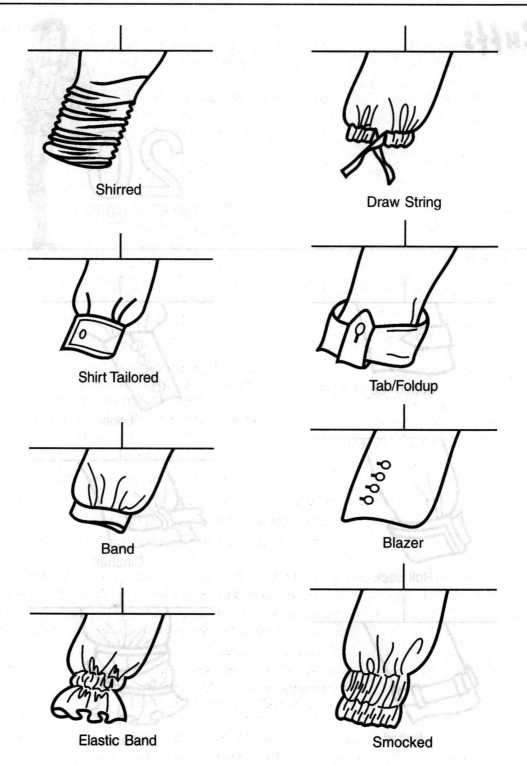

Shirred

Draw String

Shirt Tailored

Tab/Foldup

Band

Blazer

Elastic Band

Smocked

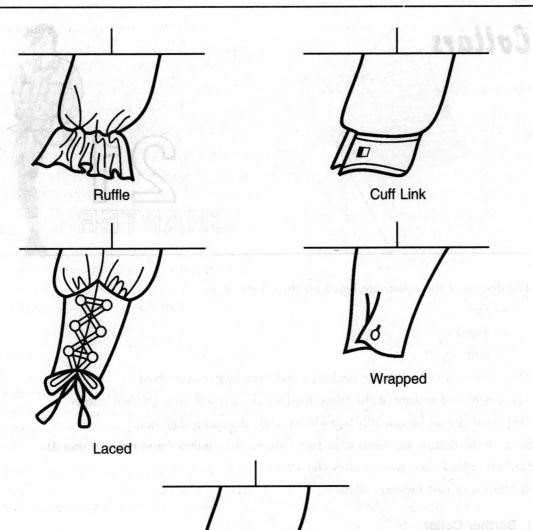

Ruffle

Cuff Link

Laced

Wrapped

Pleated

Collars

21
CHAPTER

The designs of the collars are based on three basic styles.

— Flat

— Stand

— Roll

They may be attached to the necklines and detached or converted.

The weight and texture of the fabric used for designs will give different effects.

This point should be carefully considered while designing sketches.

Some of the designs are taken from past fashions from military and national dresses.

Example: Manderian, poets, sailors and so on.

Illustration of past fashion collars.

1. Barther Collar

It is 1920's imitation of a short shoulder of a cape.

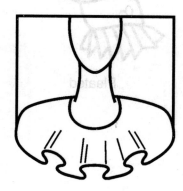

2. Gladstone Collar

A standing collar with long points worn with a scarf tied made of silk. It was famous in 19th century by the late Prime Minister of America named E. Gladstone.

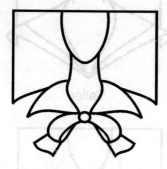

3. Quaker Collar

This collar is a flat broad turned down collar.

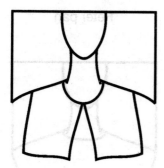

4. Funnel Collar

This collar flairs out wards at the top of the neckline opening at the siders or back. (Some-times). It is seen in pullover very often.

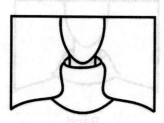

5. Poets Collar

A collar made from a soft fabric attached to a shirt/blouse. It is often worn by the famous European poets called Byson, Kiets and Shelly.

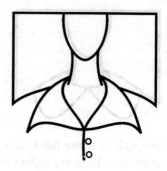

6. Sailors Collar

A collar which is squared at the back and nar-row at the front worn by sailors.

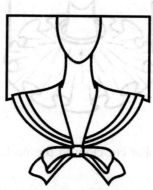

Front view

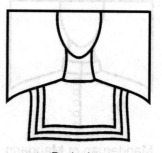

Back view

7. Eton Collar

A large collar made from a stiffen white fabric worn by the students of Eton College.

8. Pierrot Collar

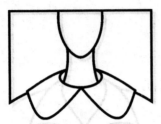

A very wide rough of white fabric has worn by French pantomime character called pierrot .

9. Manderian or Mandarin Collar

A small collar cut close to the neck.

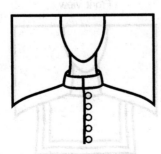

Manderuan or Mandarin

COLLARS

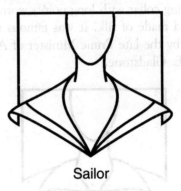

Sailor

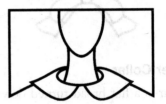

Peter pan

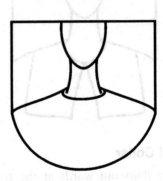

Bertha

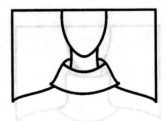

Band

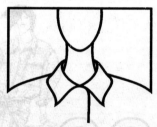

Convertible (Closed)

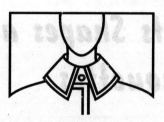

Spread Tie Collar

Open/Manila Collar

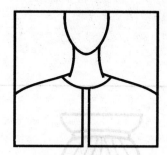

Pilgrim

Shawl

Mandarin

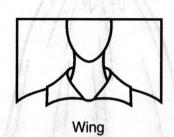

Wing

Skirts Shapes and Silhouettes

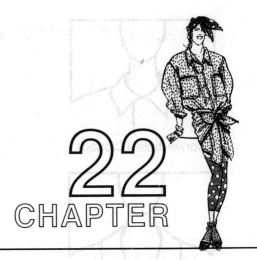

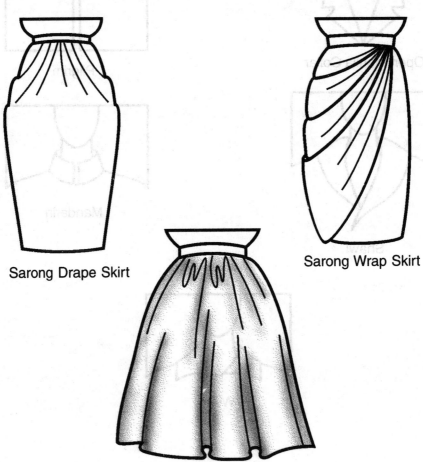

Sarong Drape Skirt

Sarong Wrap Skirt

Full Skirt (Gathered)

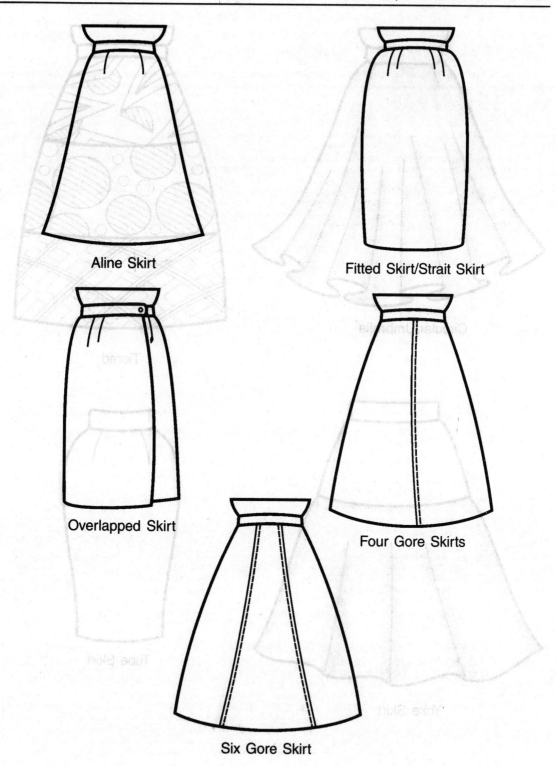

Aline Skirt

Fitted Skirt/Strait Skirt

Overlapped Skirt

Four Gore Skirts

Six Gore Skirt

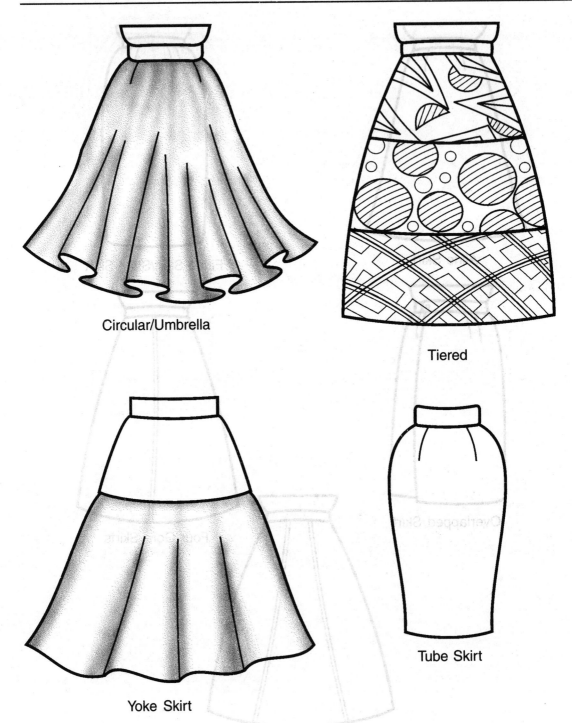

Circular/Umbrella

Tiered

Yoke Skirt

Tube Skirt

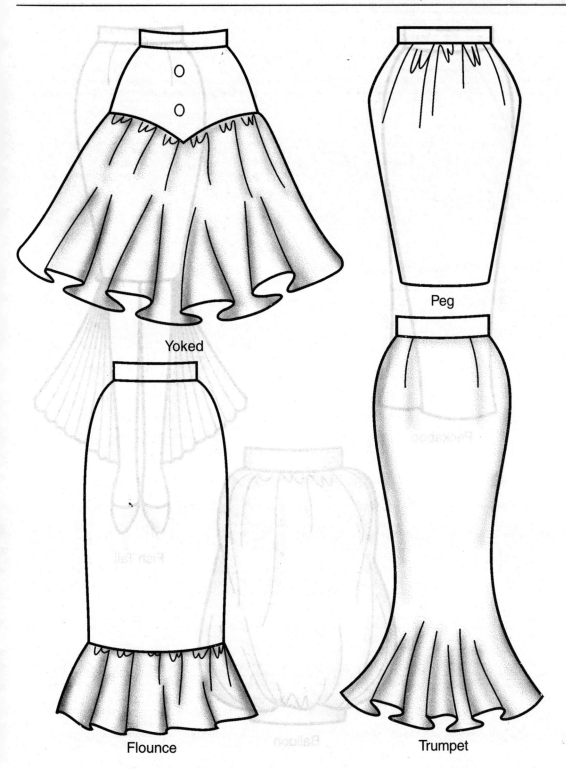

Yoked

Peg

Flounce

Trumpet

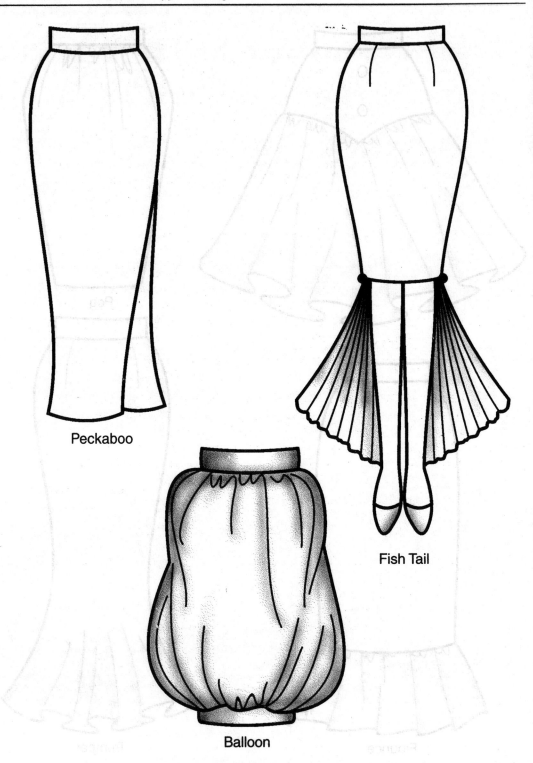

Peckaboo

Balloon

Fish Tail

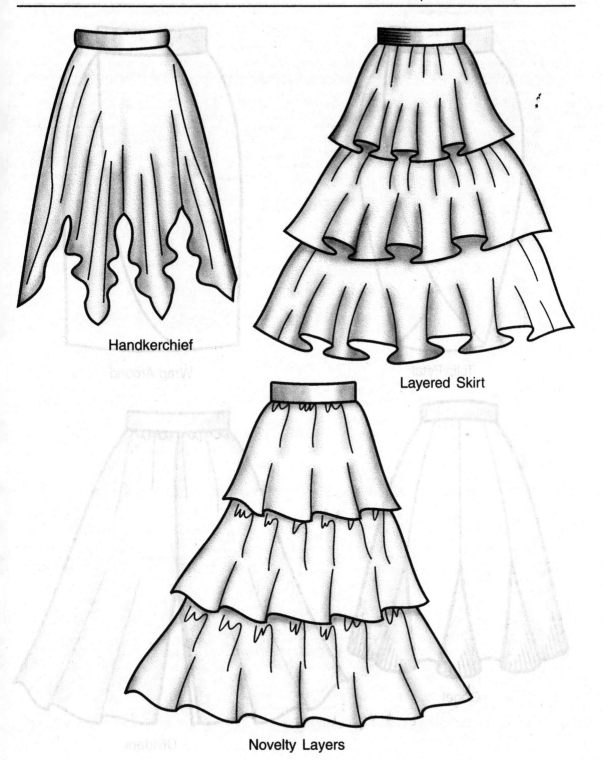

Handkerchief

Layered Skirt

Novelty Layers

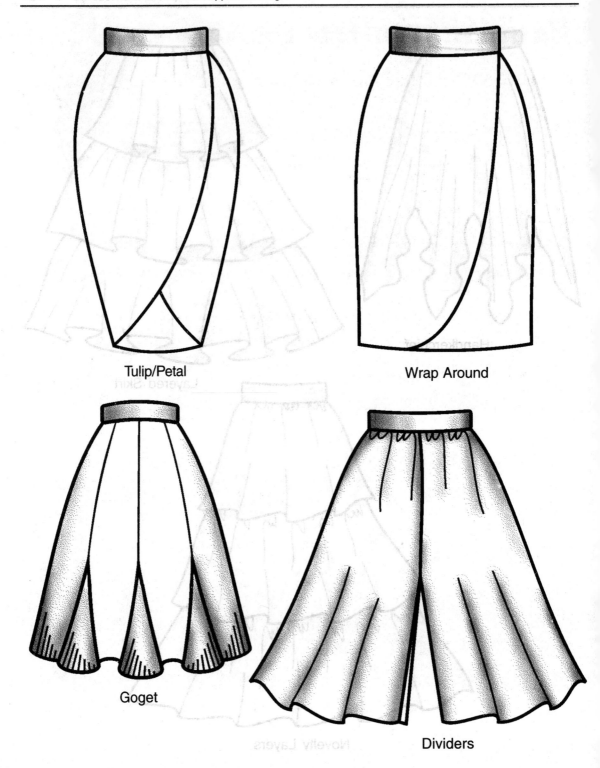

Tulip/Petal

Wrap Around

Goget

Dividers

Basic Silhouettes

Tank Top

Bandeau

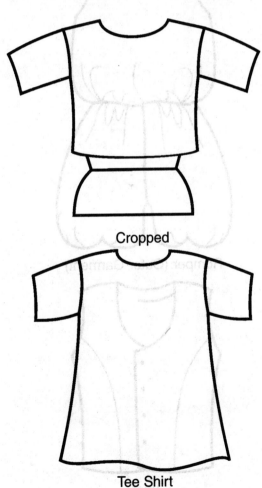

Cropped

Tee Shirt

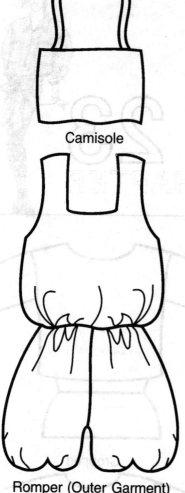

Camisole

Romper (Outer Garment)

Vest

Teddy (Under Garment)

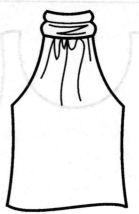

Halter

Weskit

Bustier

Polo Shirt

Camp Shirt

Empire

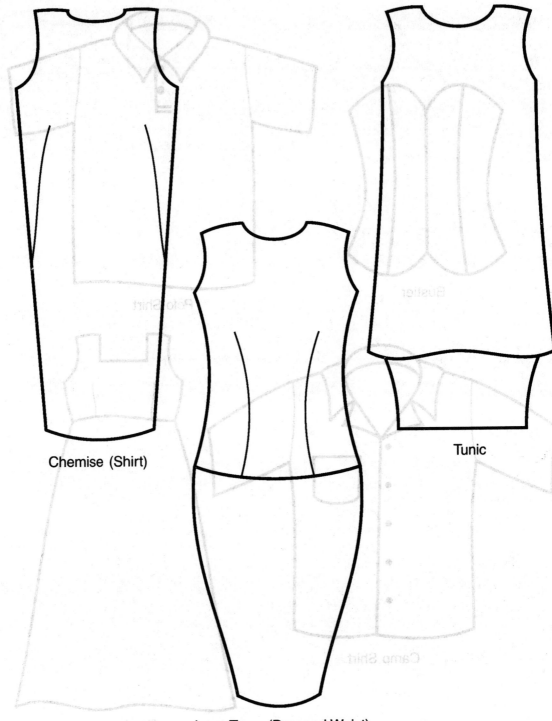

Chemise (Shirt)

Tunic

Long Torso (Dropped Waist)

Shirt Waist

Sheath

Princess Line

Blouson

Tent/Trapeze (Aline)

Blazer

Cardigan

Smoking Jacket

Bellboy Jacket

Eisenhower Jacket

Bolero

Norfolk Jacket

Peacoat (Reefer)

Safari Jacket

Redingote

Chesterfield

Wrap Coat

Cape

Tent/Trapeze

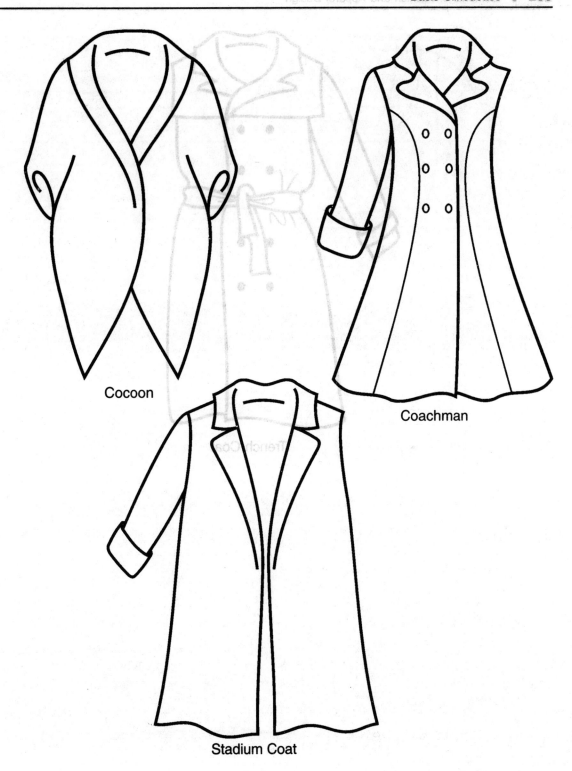

Cocoon

Coachman

Stadium Coat

Trench Coat

Pants

24
CHAPTER

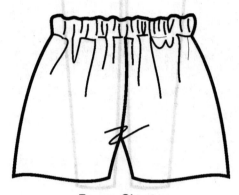

Boxer Shorts

Walking Shorts

Capri Pants

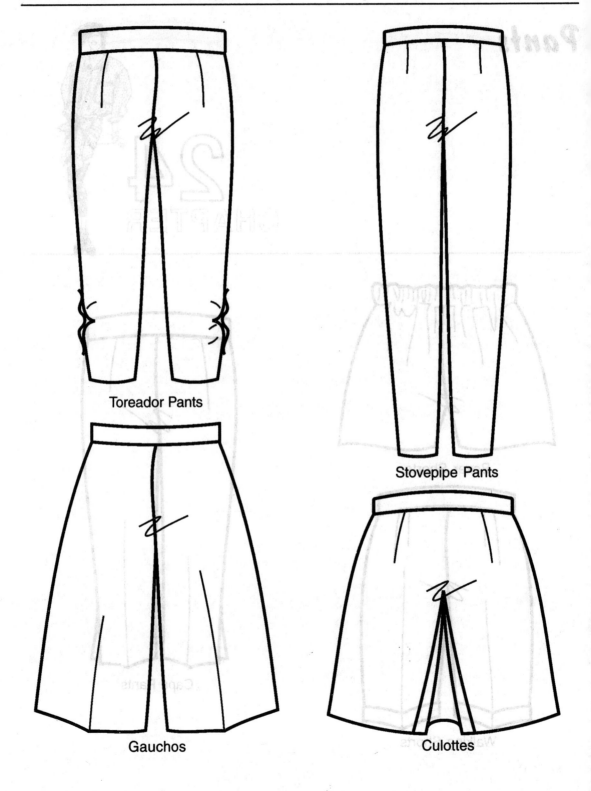

Toreador Pants

Stovepipe Pants

Gauchos

Culottes

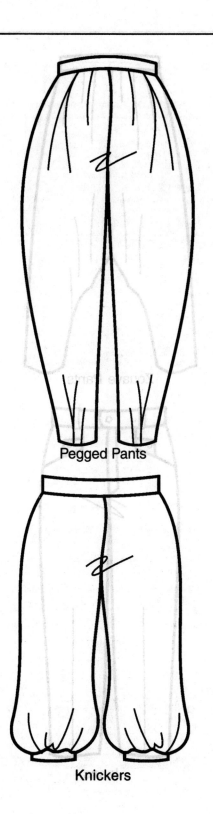

Pegged Pants

Knickers

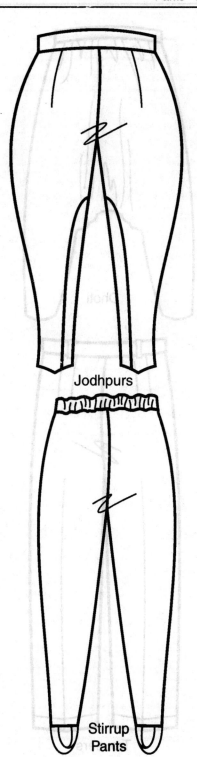

Jodhpurs

Stirrup Pants

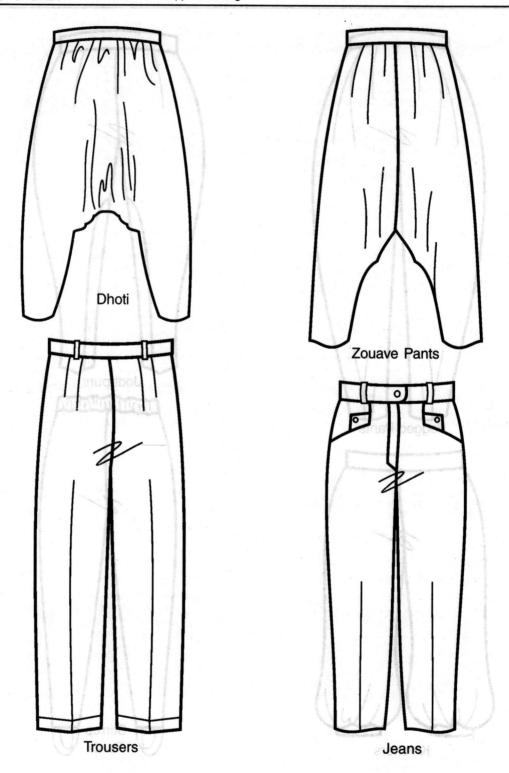

Dhoti

Zouave Pants

Trousers

Jeans

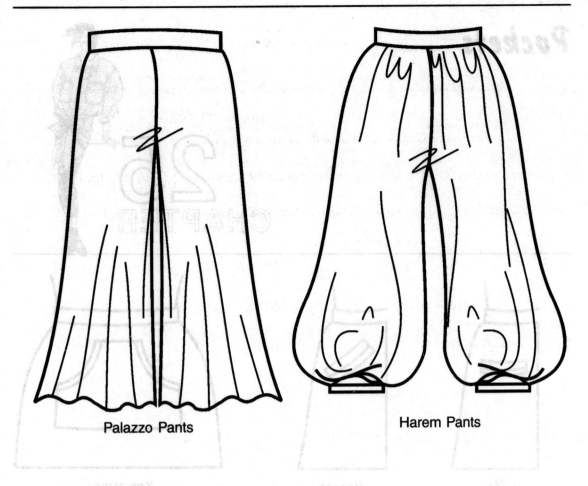

Palazzo Pants

Harem Pants

Pockets

25
CHAPTER

Welt

Besom

Kangaroo

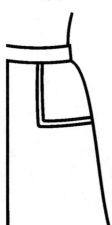

Cargo

Western

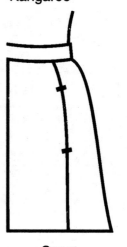

Seam

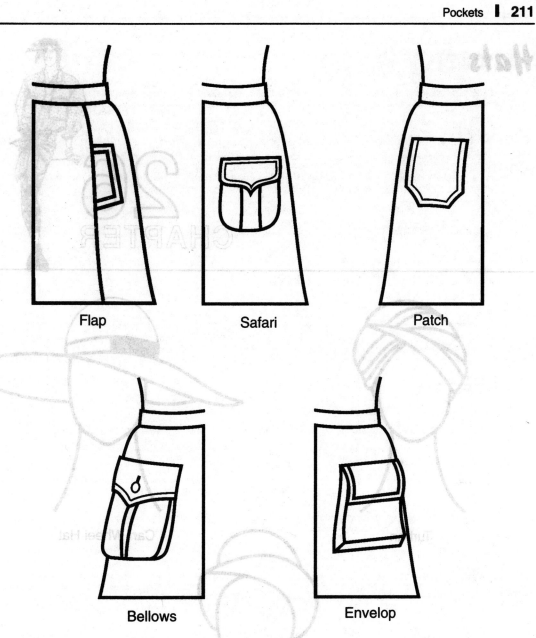

Flap

Safari

Patch

Bellows

Envelop

Hats

26
CHAPTER

Turban

Cart Wheel Hat

Cloche

Boater

Fedora

Cowboy/Western Hat

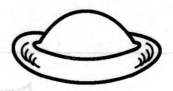

Bumper

Beret

Pillbox Hat

Navy Hat

Waist Bands

27
CHAPTER

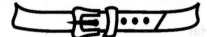

Buckle

Peplum

Cinch/D-bar Buckle

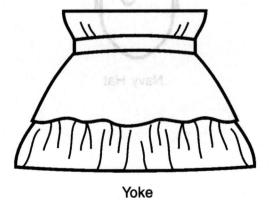

Yoke

Cummer Bund

Obi

Twist Belt

Wrap Belt

Hip Belt

Horseshoe Belt

Laced Belt

Bows and Ties

28
CHAPTER

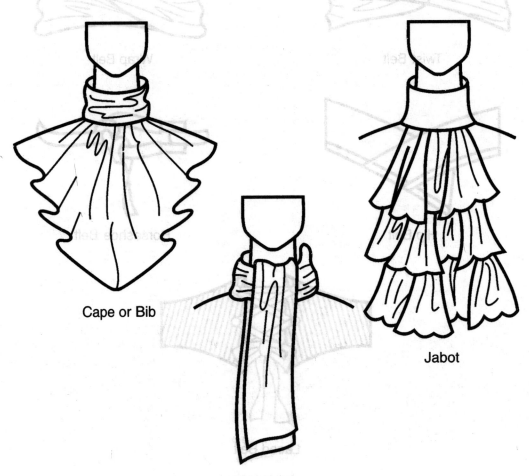

Cape or Bib

Stock Tie

Jabot

Bow

Ribbon

String

Bustle Bow

Bow

String

Ribbon

Bustle Bow